VOICE PRODUCTION AND SPEECH

BY

GRETA COLSON

Principal Lecturer in charge of Voice, Middlesex Polytechnic
Co-founder, The New College of Speech and Drama
Formerly Professor, Royal Academy of Music—Speech and Drama Faculty
Examiner for:
Licentiate of Royal Academy of Music
Associated Board of Royal Schools of Music
Adjudicator for:
British Federation of Music Festivals (Speech and Drama)
FRSAMD, FNCSD, CSSD, LRAM, LGSM, IPA Certificate

Third Edition

PITMAN

PITMAN BOOKS LIMITED
128 Long Acre, London WC2E 9AN

Associated Companies
Pitman Publishing Pty Ltd, Melbourne
Pitman Publishing New Zealand Ltd, Wellington

Second edition (under Pitman imprint) 1973
First paperback edition 1973
Reprinted 1974, 1977, 1979
Third edition 1982
Reprinted 1983

Text set in 10/12 pt Linotron 202 Times, printed and bound in Great Britain at The Pitman Press, Bath

ISBN 0 273 01841 8

PREFACE

THE terms used in Voice Theory and Speech Training are inherited from singing teachers, borrowed from physics, adapted from phonetics, dictated by physiology and born in the imagination of speech teachers. Contemporary advances in technical knowledge of the subject have added further complications.

It is not surprising that writers on the subject exhibit considerable inconsistency both in the particular terms they employ and in the meanings they attach to these. For even the enlightened teacher the task of guiding students through this labyrinth is an exacting one.

A clear presentation of the language used in teaching speech and voice is therefore of primary concern and this book is intended to provide an introductory course for students and others interested in the subject.

Thanks are due to Dr Wilfred Barlow for help on posture problems, to John Colson for advice on phonological aspects and to Bruce Morrison for practical music assistance.

My thanks are also due to the following for allowing their work to be reproduced:

George MacBeth and Macmillan's for the *Clapping Poem* on page 84
David Owen-Bell and Angela Konrad for *Down by the Mersey* on page 85
David Owen-Bell for *Call it Aloud* on page 85 and *The Gale* on page 85
Bob Cobbing for the poems on pages 86–90

CONTENTS

ILLUSTRATIONS

KEY WORDS FOR VOWEL SOUNDS

PHONETIC symbols are not used in this book. The following key words, however, have been provided. The operative sound is in italics in each instance.

PURE VOWELS

H*EE*D

H*I*D

H*EA*D

H*A*D

H*EAR*D

*A*BOUT

H*U*T

H*AR*D

H*O*CK

H*AW*K

H*OO*K

H*OO*T

VOWEL GLIDES (DIPHTHONGS)

H*ERE*

H*ARE*

T*OUR*

H*AY*

H*IGH*

H*OW*

H*OY*

H*OE*

Some speakers use also H*OAR* instead of H*AW*K in words such as 'door'.
Most speakers use a vowel glide in F*IRE* and FL*OWER* rather than giving such words two syllables.

INTRODUCTION

This book is divided into sections under the following headings:

Part I: Breath

Part II: Note

Part III: Tone

Part IV: Word

These four stages in the production of voice and speech may be tabulated as shown below.

(This plan must be read from the bottom upwards: it is put in this way in accordance with the position of the anatomical features involved. The whole physical process is initiated by the Breath, which is largely controlled by the action of the diaphragm, and culminates in the Word, which is formed in the front of the mouth.)

PHONOLOGY	*ANATOMY*	*PHYSICS*	*FUNCTION*	*CONTROL*
4. Word	Speech Organs	Particular Resonance	Particular Quality	(*a*) Ear (*b*) Muscular Sensation
3. Tone	Nose Mouth Neck	General Resonance	General Quality	(*a*) Ear (*b*) Muscular Sensation
2. Note	Vocal Folds	Vibrator (Frequency)	Pitch	Ear, in conjunction with mental image of sound required
1. Breath	Lungs	Excitor (Amplitude)	Capacity and Control	Diaphragm in association with abdominal muscles and ribs operated by intercostal muscles

PART I: BREATH

SUMMARY

Breath enters and leaves the body in accordance with the alternate increase and decrease of the size of the chest (and hence of the size of the lungs, which expand and contract according to the size of the chest itself). These changes in the size of the chest are brought about by muscular contraction and relaxation. It is the *contraction* of the intercostal muscles which moves the ribs upwards and outwards, and the *contraction* of the muscle fibres of the diaphragm which moves its central tendon downwards and makes it less dome-shaped. Thus the size of the chest is increased (*a*) laterally and (*b*) vertically; in both cases by an active muscular contraction. Breathing out is the result of relaxation of the muscles but in speech it must be controlled relaxation. In vocalization the outgoing breath interacts with the vibrating vocal folds. These impart to it the waves which after passing through the resonator are heard by the ear of the listener as 'sound'.

THE STRUCTURE OF THE CHEST (OR THORAX)

(*A*) *BONE* forms a cage which protects the upper part of the body. The SPINE, or backbone, is made up of a series of vertebrae. From the twelve dorsal vertebrae pairs of ribs pass down and round rising in the front to make a complete closure with the sternum.

Feel these on your own spine. Trace the ribs round. Feel the sweep of each rib.

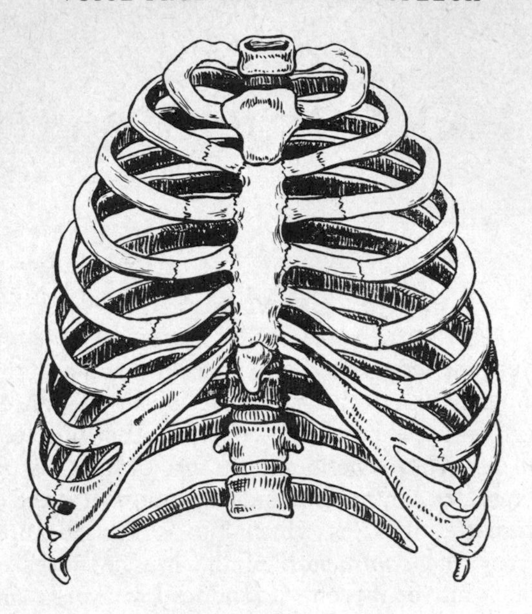

The bones of the thorax

Counting from the top:

The first seven pairs of ribs join with the sternum.

The next three pairs join with the seventh.

Two pairs are floating (they are free at the front end).

Place your hands on your waist at the side. The free ends are just above it.

Elasticity is given because the join between bone and bone (i.e. rib and sternum) is completed with cartilage, which is softer than bone.

(*B*) *MUSCLE* enables bone to move. A muscle can move in two ways only. It can contract (and so grow shorter, bringing bone towards bone) and it can cease to contract and so return to its original position.

Muscle can be seen when raw meat is cut. 'A muscle' consists of many muscle fibres and these fibres form a tough, solid sheet.

Muscles begin at one stable bone position (point of origin) and end at a second bone (point of insertion).

The Breathing Muscles

Each rib is raised towards the one above, extending the rib cage and so making the chest larger. The muscles that contract to raise the ribs are the Intercostals (between ribs). There are two sets of intercostals; the Internal and External.

The central and lower ribs have a large movement. They are relatively free and have a different shape from that of the upper ribs. This makes them move Outwards as well as upwards when one rib is raised towards the one above.

You can feel these muscles between your ribs making the rib wall solid. Now feel the lower ribs at the back where there should be an outward and upward movement. After this place your hands on the ribs just below the shoulders in front where the movement can be felt but is slight because the ribs have less freedom. When you breathe the shoulders should ride easily and the whole chest should be filled. The shoulders should never be rigid.

There is a strong muscle which divides the thorax and the abdomen. It is the Diaphragm. The muscle fibres originate at the lower edge of the ribs, the point of the sternum and the vertebrae. They then rise in a dome shape and insert into a flat, trefoil shaped central tendon. This central tendon cannot contract, so it is a stable factor and is moved only by the contraction of the muscle fibres of the diaphragm.

In passive breathing the intake is due to the diaphragm descending so making the chest space larger. This may involve a slight movement of the lower ribs. The movement is a gentle one and the diaphragm descends on average an inch to an inch and a half.

The diaphragm cannot be felt but the effect of its rise and fall can be felt if you place your hand on the arch between the ribs in front (epigastrium). When the diaphragm descends the epigastrium moves outwards; it moves back to its original position as the diaphragm ascends.

When more breath is needed rib movement is involved. This pulls the edges of the diaphragm outwards and reduces the domed shape as shown below.

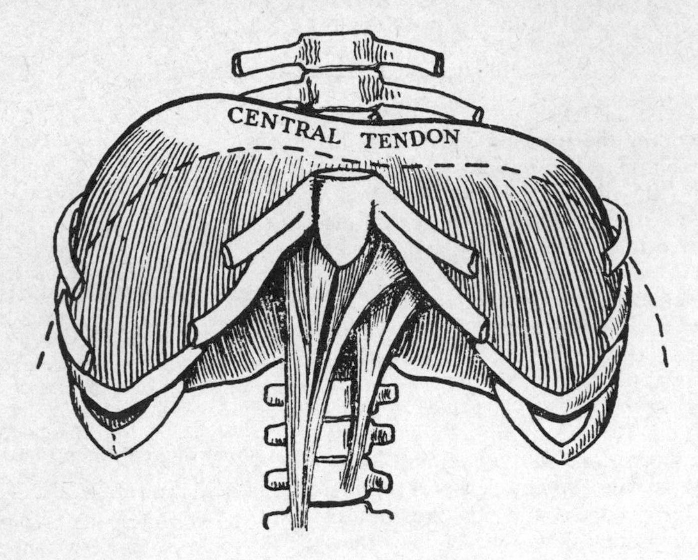

Diagram of the diaphragm

The dotted line shows the descent of the central tendon on the outward and upward movement of the ribs.

PASSAGE OF THE BREATH

The breath enters through the

MOUTH OR NOSE.
It passes down through the

PHARYNX (or neck) and has a free passage through the

LARYNX into the

TRACHEA. This is the windpipe and leads from the larynx in the neck into the thorax. It subdivides into two

BRONCHI which enter the two lungs, branch and there subdivide into minute tubes ending in air-sacs in the

LUNGS. These with the heart fill the thoracic cavity. The right lung has an upper, middle and lower lobe. The left an upper and lower. The lungs are conical in shape and follow the shape of the inside of the thorax. When the chest is enlarged the lungs follow its new shape.

Realization that the lungs are made up of separate lobes may make taking a full breath an easier process.

THE ORDER OF THE BREATHING PROCESS

Breathing is primarily for supplying oxygen to the blood. When the amount of carbon dioxide in the blood stream reaches a certain tension the breathing muscles are stimulated into contracting.

1. The muscles contract enlarging the chest cavity and
2. The breath passes into the lungs equalizing the pressure between the air in the lungs and the air outside.
3. The muscles cease to contract and the chest cavity returns to its original size and
4. The breath passes out as the size of the lungs is reduced, so equalizing the pressure between the air in the lungs and the air outside.

During gentle breathing only about one-tenth of the total amount of air in the lungs passes in and out. This is known as TIDAL AIR. The amount of tidal air can be considerably increased at will but nearly half the air always remains in the lungs and is known as RESIDUAL AIR. About a quarter remains even after very forceful breathing out.

Breath can be given more capacity and control by:

1. FULL CHEST BREATH. The ribs are moved outwards and upwards and the diaphragm descends so enlarging the chest in circumference and length. The continued alternation between contraction and relaxation of the muscles gives a rhythmical rise and fall to the ribs.

Keeping your shoulders spread, see page 19(*d*), place your right hand on the left sixth and seventh ribs. The rib movement can be felt.

2. Rib Reserve Breathing. The ribs are extended and held in this position. The diaphragm continues to contract and cease to do so independently. This ensures plenty of air in the chest throughout the procedure and helps the tone to be steady and secure. The breath can be taken quickly and silently through the mouth. The ribs being extended helps the position of the larynx.

Keep one hand on the ribs and place the other on the abdominal wall in the arch between the ribs. The ribs stay out but the movement of the diaphragm can be felt by the movement of the abdominal muscles forming the body wall in the arch between the ribs. These move out when the breath enters the chest and in when the breath passes out. This is especially clear if you keep your ribs out and then pant gently.

The movement of the upper Abdominal Muscles in breathing is antagonistic to that of the diaphragm. As the diaphragm descends the upper abdominal muscles lose contraction allowing the slight forward bulge of the upper abdominal wall. As the diaphragm ascends and the breath passes out the abdominal muscles contract and the abdominal wall reverts to its previous position.

The word 'antagonist' in its technical sense implies cooperation rather than opposition.

BREATHING AND VOCAL PRACTICE

Vocal practice should be undertaken when one is feeling fresh and lively and should not be crammed into the day's activity as a matter of conscience.

POSTURE

The whole body is involved in the production of vocal sound so practice begins with posture. Unfortunately, when man became upright, balancing his weight on the two relatively small triangles of his feet, he immediately increased the tension in his muscles which affected posture and vocal production.

An important muscle area for speakers is found at the back of the neck where muscular contraction tilts back the head, sticks out the chin and impairs the laryngeal functioning. Before speaking with any power, most people contract these muscles. To correct the fault, deliberately relax these muscles. Break the habit by beginning to speak only when you are muscularly ready: rushing into vocalization means encouraging poor usage. Check yourself carefully in a front plus side mirror for the following posture faults.

(*a*) Placing weight unevenly to left or right.
(*b*) Pulled in and unevenly positioned shoulders.
(*c*) Head tilted to right or left; or head pulled back with chin drawn in; or head thrust forward with chin out.
(*d*) Spine not lengthening: spine curving excessively in lumbar area hollowing back: left or right curves.
(*e*) A pulled-in thorax: rigidity in this area.

(Refer, too, to past photographs.)

Resolving Posture Difficulties

The following exercises are based on the Alexander Technique.

(*a*) Supine Position. Follow the directions on page 21.
(*b*) Monkey Position. Stand with your feet set fairly widely apart. Bend your knees a little keeping feet and knees out. Bring your head, neck and trunk forward in one line until your head is over your feet. This is a good position in which to further the experience of breathing as it exposes the lower back ribs, a vital area. The position is hard on the legs, so when you wish, come up in two stages, first the trunk and head, then straighten the legs. Continue letting energy go up through your body.
(*c*) Sit, keeping your spine lengthening and coming up from the chair. Do not sink down into it. Do not lean against the back of the chair. Stand by unbending your knees and do not lurch forward. Sail up and have the sensation of continuing to go up. Sit, by reversing the process.
(*d*) Stretch out your arms sideways, ease your shoulders and think

them out. Continue to do this taking your time, and as the shoulders cease to pull in the arms will elongate.

(*e*) Sit, keeping your length and spreading your shoulders. Then come forward with the lower trunk, hold the position, then go back with the upper trunk appreciating the way the guts lift.

(*f*) Spread the shoulders and then encourage the sensation of the shoulder girdle dropping back over the rib cage. At the same time think of energy rising up the spine.

(*g*) Keep the length of your body and walk, carried by a movement from the hip joints. Do not let the knees bend or the pelvis come into play.

(*h*) Throughout your body think bone away from bone; let your body energize outwards, do not hug yourself in.

(*i*) Good body usage applies to all human activities, not only to specific undertakings.

(*j*) Terminology: LENGTHEN NOT SHORTEN. HEAD: FORWARD AND UP NOT BACK AND DOWN. SPREAD NOT DRAWN IN.

FURTHER PHYSICAL PREPARATION

Think and work through the posture ideas before going on to general and specific body exercises. Remain aware of good usage and stop to check whenever necessary.

Begin with broad and rhythmical whole body work. Move freely and lightly in the available space. First use music as a stimulus then discard it and establish your own rhythm. See your body as a mobile in space and experiment with the patterns it can make, varying style from the strong and bold to the smooth and lyrical. Then work through parts of the body.

(I) FEET AND LEGS

The legs are swung freely from the hip, the knees made flexible and the ankles and parts of the foot moved. Energy passes into the feet and up into the body. When standing, the weight should be evenly balanced between the feet and slightly back on the heels; knees must not be tensed, neither may they sag; lightness of movement should be the aim. All foot exercises should be done either in unblocked practice shoes or with bare feet. Refer to page 19, posture fault (*a*).

(II) The Trunk

The waist should be made flexible with various bending and twisting movements. The spine needs special attention; the back lengthening and widening gives a sensation of rising energy. The small of the back must be easy so that there is no undue hollowing. Consider pages 19–20, faults (*d*)(*e*). Try the following:

Lie with the back on the floor with a book about two inches thick supporting the head so that the spine, neck and head are aligned. Place the heels eighteen inches or so apart and allow the feet to rotate outwards; the arms lie easily by the sides palms downwards. Achieve physical and mental ease.

Keep the knees apart and bend the knees, letting the feet travel along the ground towards the body until they are under the knees. The whole spine should now be straight and moulded to the floor. If there is still a curve in the lumbar region and this part of the spine does not touch the floor do not force it down but bring the knees together and up towards the chin so that the spine is now touching the floor. Now let the legs go back slowly to the previous position, maintaining the contact between the spine and the floor in the lumbar region. Whilst in this position cultivate the sense of lengthening and widening the back with the shoulders flat on the floor and the neck lifting with rising energy away from the rest of the spine. No movement is needed; just observe the sensation. Let the feet slide outwards again; the curve in the lumbar region will reassert itself. One object of this exercise is to correct excessive lumbar curvature. The sensation of the straight back when the legs are bent should be appreciated and remembered.

Repeat the same exercise but in a vertical position against a wall. Place the feet about eighteen inches apart with the toes pointed out at an angle of forty-five degrees and the heels about two inches from the wall. Let the body move back in one piece from the ankles against the wall. If the posture is correct shoulders and buttocks touch the wall at the same time. Let the knees travel forwards and outwards over the toes so that the body slides down the wall about one foot. The whole spine should now make contact with the wall in the same way as when the knees were bent in the supine position on the floor. If it does not, this is an indication that the habitual poise involves excessive lumbar curvature. Regular practice of this exercise on the floor and then against the wall helps to remedy this. As in the previous exercise when the correct position is achieved the sensation should be remembered so that it gradually becomes part of one's body image. As the knees travel forwards and outwards a sensation that the head is remaining up in the air and that the body is lengthening is experienced; the thought should not be of a downward movement. The head must not be allowed to fall back so that it touches the wall. When coming up again the sensation is not one of pressing upwards with the feet or the knees but rather of the head rising effortlessly, as if it were lighter than air, and the rest of the body following. When the body is erect there will of course be some curve in the lumbar region. Only excessive curvature is undesirable as it voids the supporting of the back by the lower ribs. Slumping in a seated position is another bad habit to be avoided.

(iii) Shoulders, Arms and Hands

The roll of the shoulders has to be felt well within the body. The shoulders form a cross with the spine and balance on either side of it in a see-saw action. There should be a feeling of the shoulders branching from the spine; the arms should turn out from the shoulder, with elbows out, wrists in, hands out. Arms and hands should be exercised in all possible directions, strong aggressive movements alternating with slow or rapid delicate ones. Bear in mind page 19 fault (*b*) and pages 19–20(*d*)(*f*).

Particular attention has to be given to the shoulders in breathing. Rigidity must be avoided so that when the lungs fill to a good capacity the shoulders ride easily. There should be no hint of holding them down to prevent them 'rising'. It is particularly important to refer to this point because of the old trick children have of shrugging the shoulders to emphasize that they have obligingly taken in a breath as requested. A tense upper chest can be caused by over-correcting this fault.

(IV) NECK AND HEAD

Ease is needed for neck and head exercises. Special attention should be given to the set of the head (see page 19 fault (*c*)). The head position begins at the feet and energy rising up through the body balances the head in the way a ball balances on a jet of water. Common faults are drooping shoulders and a poked forward head. The well-positioned column of the neck is a vital point of posture. The head and neck have to be regarded as free and mobile and not as being set in a fixed position. The spine, shoulders and neck interact to ensure the open throat position needed for good voice production.

BREATHING

The first step in the acquisition of full breath and able control is to become aware of the functioning of your chest, especially the sensation of breathing and the action of the muscles. Find out what happens when you cough, groan, sigh, lift a heavy object, run half a mile or are scared stiff. When approaching formal exercises consider the following points:

(*a*) If the body usage is good, formal exercises aid conscious control but may be kept to a minimum.
(*b*) There should never be undue physical demand made on anyone during breathing exercises. The aim should be a gradual increase of capacity and control while avoiding any strain.
(*c*) The output is as important as the intake. In the exercises described the breath should be allowed to flow out freely but timed to the number of counts.
(*d*) It is possible to lay too much emphasis on capacity. Frequent intake is not a fault so long as it is related to sense and is unobtrusive.

(*e*) A rigid chest should be guarded against: the aim throughout all breathing work is to keep the chest flexible. Rigidity and flexibility are both reflected in vocal tone.
(*f*) In breathing, as in all voice work, there must be no hasty rushing into it: physical confidence and mental understanding should precede the action.

It is an advantage to begin breathing practice on the floor, preferably in the position described on page 21. In this position the ease of the body may be checked and a lengthened spread sensation encouraged. The back of the neck needs special attention to ensure the muscles 'let go' and the root of the tongue should feel free. When air enters the lungs, it sometimes helps to imagine it enters through the eighth, ninth, tenth and eleventh back ribs. (Dr Wilfred Barlow described this as the 'gill' position.) The slight fall of the sternum during expiration is more easily discerned in this position.

Up to the age of around fourteen breathing exercises should not be formal. At this age full chest breathing may be taught. This improves the capacity of the breathing and imposes a simple control. The first five exercises establish this.

When not using the breath for speech the cycle of gentle effortless breathing is a slow intake, a slightly quicker output and then a pause. This cycle has to be altered when demands are going to be made on the breath. The first exercise equalizes the time of intake and the time of output.

1. Breathe in to a mental count of *In,2,3*.
   Breathe *Out,2,3*.
   (Repeat a few times).

   In this and the following exercises vocalize the repeats.

The time of intake is gradually reduced and the time of output increased.

2. Breath *In,2,3*.
   Breathe *Out,2,3,4,5,6*.
   Rest,*2,3*.
3. Breathe *In*, quickly but smoothly.
   Breathe *Out,2,3,4,5,6*.

Further control of the breath is the next step.

4. Breathe *In,2,3,4,5,6*.
   Breathe *Out,2,3* Pause.
   Breathe *Out,2,3*.

In these exercises care must be taken that there is no closure of the air passages. The pause must be made by maintaining a stationary position of the ribs and diaphragm.

5. Breathe *In*, quickly but smoothly.
   Breathe *Out,2,3* pause.
   Out,2,3, pause.
   Out,2,3.

RIB RESERVE BREATHING gives further control and is useful to professional voice users. Success depends on an easy thorax. See page 19 faults (*d*)(*e*), page 20(*e*)(*f*)(*h*). It should not supersede full chest breathing for meeting extra vocal demands but is a valuable alternative. In rib reserve breathing a full chest breath is taken and then the ribs are held in an extended position. The diaphragm continues to move independently, contracting and going back to its original position, thus continuing the breathing process.

In this exercise the ribs are held out and the sensation of doing this should be recognized and carried into the following exercises. The exercise is to establish the feeling of holding the ribs in the extended position needed for rib reserve breathing.

Again, avoid a glottal closure during this exercise.

6. Breathe *In,2,3.*
   Pause,*2,3* (with the ribs held out).
   Breathe *Out,2,3.*
   Rest,*2,3.*
   (Repeat a few times).

Having learnt to hold the ribs out the next exercise is to learn the sensation of the diaphragm moving whilst the ribs remain in an extended position.

There should not be a false thrusting in and out of the epigastrium (the part of the body lying between the arch of the ribs).

7. Breathe *In*, taking a good chest breath.
   Keep the ribs held out and with only the diaphragm and abdominal muscles moving pant very gently through the open mouth being careful to ensure that the movement of the abdominal wall is correlated with the intake and output of the breath. At the end of the exercise Breathe *Out*, letting the ribs come in.

The movement of the diaphragm can now be extended so that the time of diaphragmatic intake and output is prolonged.

8. Breathe *In*, taking a good chest breath.
   Keep the ribs held out and continue breathing with the diaphragm only working. Take the breath in and out through the mouth.
   Breathe *Out,2,3.*
   Breathe *In,2,3.*
   Breathe *Out,2,3* etc.
   Finally breathe out and let the ribs come in.

Finally there should be a full rib reserve breathing exercise.

9. Breathe *In*, taking a good chest breath.
   Hold the ribs out and with the diaphragm and abdominal muscles only working, Breathe *Out,2,3.*
   Renew the breath rapidly and gently through the mouth.
   Repeat several times.
   Finally breathe out, letting the ribs come in.

Three factors to consider when rib reserve breathing is attempted:

(i) The student needs an informed teacher to monitor the learning process.

(ii) Good physical usage is essential to ensure an easy thorax. Without it, thoracic tension already present will increase and tone will be hard and inflexible.

(iii) Rib reserve breathing should not replace full chest breathing with the ribs moving instead of being held in an extended position. It should complement it.

Its advantages are not only in extra control and muscular economy but also in security from the extra air in the lungs resulting in markedly improved tone.

FINAL IMPORTANT FACTOR APPLYING TO ALL BREATHING FOR SPEECH. The breath is taken through the nose before vocalization begins but there is a brief oral intake after the mouth opens and before sound is made.

PART II: NOTE

SUMMARY

The note of the human voice is made by breath passing through the vibrating vocal folds (sometimes called the cords). If the laryngeal note were isolated it would be scarcely audible. It has to be passed through the resonators to become recognizable. The force of the breath attacking the vocal folds is directed from the diaphragm. The breath in this case is the excitor (or striking force).

The loudness of the sound depends upon the strength of the breath force and is called VOLUME. The more breath employed the louder the sound produced.

The PITCH is imposed by the larynx and depends upon the length, mass and tenseness of the vocal folds. The longer the folds the lower the pitch; the greater the mass (thickness and weight) the lower the pitch; the tenser the folds the higher the pitch. The rule about length can be remembered if a man's larynx is compared with a woman's, and a woman's with a child's. The pitch rises in these three cases as the larynx becomes smaller. Mass can be explained by a length of elastic; the thicker it is, the lower the note when it is twanged. A piece of elastic can also demonstrate the change in pitch due to tenseness; if a certain length is pulled tight and twanged and the pitch noted, and then the same elastic is pulled tighter and twanged again, the second twang will be higher in pitch than the first because the elastic is tenser.

It is neither desirable nor advisable to think in a conscious way about the larynx and about pitch. The aim should be an accurate and vital mental conception.

THE STRUCTURE OF THE LARYNX

The larynx is situated at the top of the trachea. It is suspended from the Hyoid (tongue) Bone. Cartilages and muscles are arranged to form a long box to keep the breath passage open and protect the vocal folds.

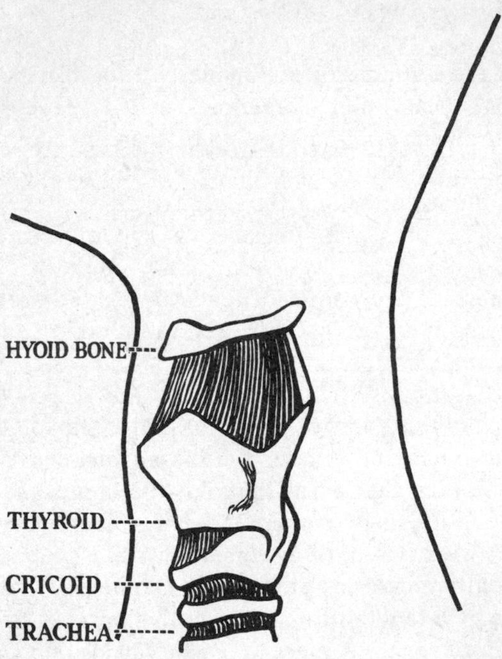

Diagram showing the position of the larynx and the protecting cartilages

The trachea is kept open by incomplete rings of cartilage. The larynx rests on a complete ring at the top of the trachea called the Cricoid Cartilage. The larynx is mainly protected by the Thyroid Cartilage which screens it in front but is open at the back. It can be seen in the neck as the 'Adam's apple'. The Epiglottis juts up over the opening of the larynx. The Glottis is the space between the Vocal Folds. These folds are the vibrator of the voice and stretch from the thyroid cartilage in front to the ARYTENOID CARTILAGES at the back. The arytenoids are triangular and are situated on the cricoid.

PHONATION

THE BREATH IS THE EXCITOR AND IT ATTACKS THE VIBRATOR (VIBRATING VOCAL FOLDS).

The nature of this vibration need not be investigated in detail. It is sufficient to know that the folds meet and part, causing a frequent stoppage in the outgoing breath stream. The effect of this repeated stoppage is that the egressive air-stream is vibrated as it passes into the resonators where it is given TONE (general quality). The vocal folds are approximated by the swivelling action of the arytenoid cartilages. When the pitch is mentally conceived the vocal folds vibrate at the frequency required to produce that note.

There are two aspects of the vocal folds which have to be considered. The first is their length; on the size of the larynx depends the overall height or depth of the voice. The second is the tension of the folds upon which variations of pitch depend. The tenser the folds the higher the pitch; the arytenoid cartilages tilt, tightening the folds.

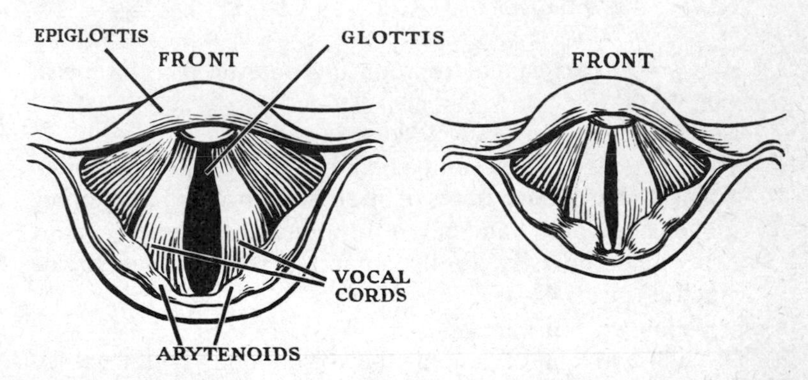

Left Diagram showing the glottis open during breathing
Right Diagram showing the glottis positioned for speaking

Note: Vocal cords are now normally called vocal folds.

THE NOTE AND VOCAL PRACTICE

Vocal practice should concentrate on a mental conception of the note. It is dangerous to be consciously aware of the working of the larynx.

The ear plays the controlling part in supplying the mental image needed to produce the note. The ear therefore must be trained and made sensitive to pitch; this training should be extended to reproducing the notes heard. Suggested instruments are Descant Recorder (possible keys C, D, G minor), Guitar and, less availably, the Flute. As well as training the ear to the individual note, scales and melodies should be sung.

The attack of the breath on the vocal folds is a danger area in voice production. Without good breath control there is a tendency to manage the breath by closing the glottis and the result is a hard vocal attack. A slurred uncertain attack is equally to be avoided. The aim is an accurately attacked and vigorously sustained note.

Although in formation note precedes tone, in practice the resonators have to be exercised before vocalized breath is used.

FAULTS OF NOTE

(i) A few speakers cannot reproduce a note or speech-tune at will.

(ii) More common is a restricted use of range.

(iii) This is sometimes accompanied by the speaker failing to establish the 'middle' notes of his or her range and developing spoken notes above and below this. Finding the 'middle' most easily made notes is closely connected with resonator scale practice (pages 42–45).

In connection with (iii) are:

(*a*) The common fault of keeping the voice too low, often caused by 'pushing down' of the larynx. It can also be due to a reluctance some men have to use the fine, higher notes of their range.

(*b*) Women often do the opposite and keep their voices too high long after lower notes have developed.

(*c*) Some women regularly pitch up a fourth or fifth when performing.

The eradication of pitch faults needs skilled guidance.

PART III: TONE

SUMMARY

The original note made in the larynx by the interaction of breath and vocal folds is modified by the resonators. The pitch is imposed by the larynx and the resonators add general resonance which is TONE. The function of the resonators is to enhance the original note, giving it body and audibility. There are three main resonators: the pharynx (or Neck), which is the first through which the vibrating air-stream passes; the mouth, lying at right angles to it and through which most of the breath passes out; the nose through which a small proportion of the breath passes out. Good tone depends upon a balance between these, each duly playing its part. This depends on the resonators being in a healthy state. In addition to producing general quality the resonators contain the speech organs which produce particular quality, i.e. individual speech sounds. When the velum is raised nasal resonance is mainly sympathetic rather than direct. The vibrating breath passing through the mouth hits the hard palate causing the air above it to vibrate. Sub-glottal (below the folds) sympathetic resonance also occurs.

THE STRUCTURE OF THE RESONATORS

THE PHARYNX

The important aspect of any resonator is that it is a hollow space. The pharynx and mouth share the ability to adjust their size and shape; the nose is constant in both size and shape.

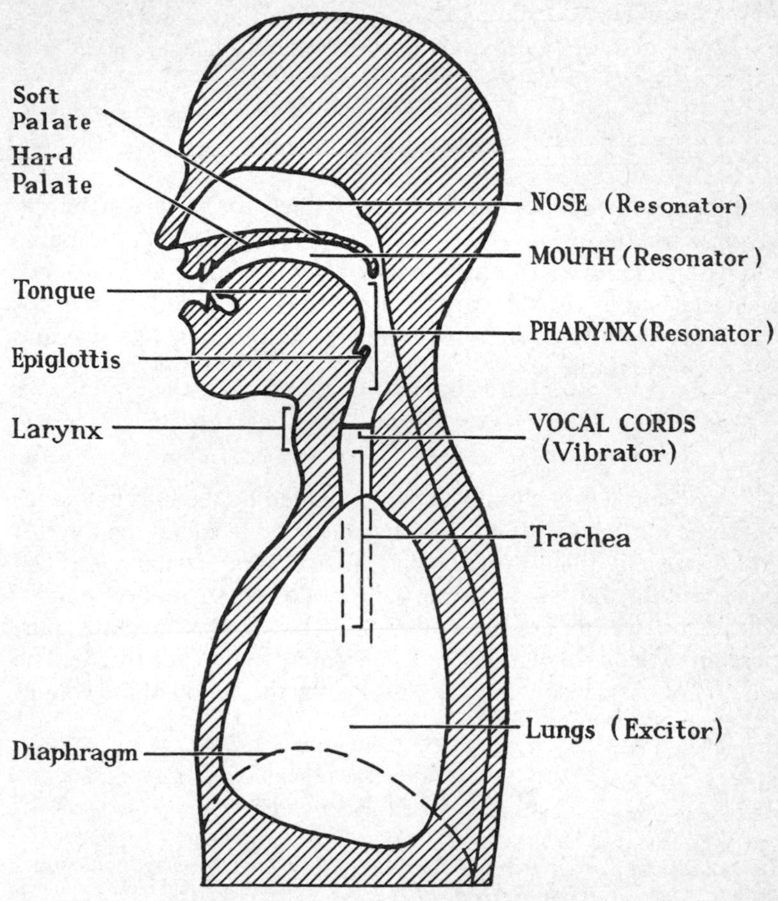

Diagrammatic view of a vertical section through the chest, pharynx, mouth and nose

Note: The size of the nasal cavity is not really as large in proportion to the other cavities as it appears to be. Much of the space is filled with convoluted bone.

The pharynx extends upwards from the larynx; it is bounded laterally by muscular walls and ends at the velum when this is raised. When this is lowered the pharynx continues into the head cavity as the naso-pharynx. It can be sub-divided into:

the LARYNGOPHARYNX, the part just above the larynx;

the OROPHARYNX, the part at the back of the mouth; and
the NASOPHARYNX, the part opposite the nasal openings.
All these parts adjust in size and shape.

THE MOUTH

The mouth is bounded at the back by the oropharynx or by the velum when this is lowered. Its base is the tongue which is capable of flexible changes. The hard palate above is stable and does not change position. In the front the mouth is bounded by the lips which are also its ORIFICE (or opening) and can change size and shape considerably.

THE NOSE

The nose consists of a hollow space bounded by the internal bones of the head. It is divided in two by a long bone called the SEPTUM and is partially filled by scroll-like bones called TURBINATES. The bones within the head are partially hollowed to reduce weight. These hollowed bones are called SINUSES. They serve little purpose in voice production and can safely be disregarded. The amount of nasal resonance is controlled by the action of the velum.

RESONANCE

When a current of air is passed through a hollow space a RESONANT PITCH is heard.

If you take a large bottle with a small neck and blow through it a particular resonant pitch will be heard. Take another bottle of a different shape and size or with a different opening and a different resonant pitch will be heard.

Each hollow space has its own resonant pitch which depends on the size and shape of the hollow space and also upon the size and number of its openings. These openings are called ORIFICES.

The hollow space most actively concerned with vowel formation is the mouth. This will be considered first:

When the jaw is dropped and the tongue is placed in various positions different vowel sounds are made. If these positions are breathed through each one will be found to have its own RESONANT PITCH in the same way that a current of air passing through any hollow space has its resonant pitch. Hollow spaces can be arranged in a sequence that enables a scale to be made of the resonant pitch.

The vowel shapes can be arranged so that the resonant pitches make a scale. Such an arrangement is known as a RESONATOR SCALE.

A series of identical bottles filled to differing heights can be hung in a sequence that results in a scale being heard when they are struck.

The sequence of the resonator scale derived from English vowel sounds begins with the back of the tongue raised close to the soft palate and the lips closely rounded. The back of the tongue lowers and the lips open progressively.

These in order are
H*OO*T
H*OO*K
H*OE*
H*AW*K
H*O*CK
H*AR*D

The central vowels come next (these are vowels made by raising the centre of the tongue).

H*U*T
H*EAR*D

Then the front of the tongue rises progressively through the next group until it is close to the hard palate and the last part of the sequence is formed.

H*A*D
H*EA*D
H*AY*
H*I*D
H*EE*D

THE SEQUENCE OF THE RESONATOR SCALE is therefore: H*OO*T H*OO*K H*OE* H*AW*K H*O*CK H*AR*D H*U*T H*EAR*D H*A*D H*EA*D H*AY* H*I*D H*EE*D
(A useful mnemonic is WHO WOULD KNOW AUGHT OF ART MUST LEARN AND THEN TAKE HIS EASE. Each word to be pronounced with its full value as in isolation.)

Vowels are breathed through in this sequence so that the resonant pitch is heard and checked. In considering TONE the resonant pitch of the neck has to be studied as well as that of the mouth.

Breathe through the sequence and hear the steady rise of the resonant pitch. It should be just audible. If friction is heard the eventual tone will be hard and restricted.

Neck (or Lower) Resonance

During the following explanation think of the mouth resonator and the neck resonator working separately and each supplying its own resonant pitch. In the following vowels H*OO*T H*OO*K H*OE* H*AW*K H*AR*D the resonant pitches of the neck and mouth are separate but identical. After H*AR*D the resonant pitch of the mouth continues to rise *but the Resonant Pitch of the Neck has a Descending Scale.* So, as the positions pass from H*AR*D to H*EE*D (H*AR*D H*U*T H*EAR*D H*A*D H*EA*D H*AY* H*I*D H*EE*D) the resonant pitch of the mouth and the resonant pitch of the neck are different *and give two separate qualities to the tone.* This neck resonance is known as Lower Resonance. Without sufficient lower resonance tone is thin and lacks body.

Neck resonance can be heard if the ears are completely covered when the resonator scale sequence is practised.

Good Tone Depends on Balanced use of Mouth, Neck and Nose Resonance

To understand the working of the human resonators in more detail two fundamental rules of resonance have to be grasped and applied:

1. The smaller the resonator the higher the pitch.
2. The smaller the orifice the lower the pitch.

The resonator scale begins with the vowel H*OO*T; the mouth orifice is small (close lip-rounding), therefore the resonant pitch is low. The lips become progressively more open as far as H*AR*D and the resonant pitch rises as the orifice becomes larger. In the neck the resonant pitch is low for H*OO*T because the orifice (the opening between the back of the tongue and the soft palate) is small. From H*OO*T to H*AR*D both the mouth and neck resonant pitch rises because both orifices become progressively larger. After H*AR*D (actually after H*U*T: see the resonator scale) the resonant pitch of the mouth continues to rise because the front of the tongue rises steadily towards the hard palate making the resonator smaller and so raising the resonant pitch. In the neck meanwhile the orifice becomes steadily smaller as the front of the tongue rises towards the hard palate and so the resonant pitch falls. By the time H*EE*D is reached the difference in the resonant pitch of the mouth and that of the neck exceeds an octave.

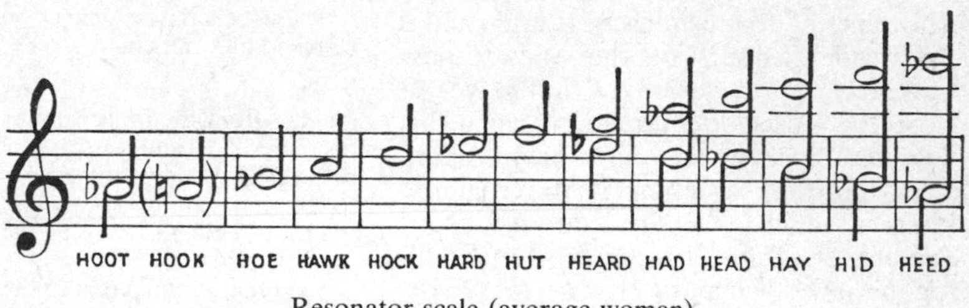

Resonator scale (average woman)

TONE AND VOCAL PRACTICE

In theory the sequence of BREATH, NOTE, TONE is a logical one. The excitor (the breath) is needed to attack the vibrator (the vocal folds) and the vibrating egressive air-stream passes through the positioned resonators receiving resonance which is tone. In practice, however, the matter is not so simple. The resonators have to acquire good habits before the note is passed through them. Such habits depend partly on muscular skill, and exercises for the speech organs (the movable parts of the resonators) have to precede exercises for positioning the resonators.

By the time tone is considered, good posture and use of the body in exercises and in breathing should have helped in the attainment of a good physiological standard. A dynamic personal image gives the voice a lively, vital quality. A depressed, unimaginative outlook works to the detriment of tone. The aim is an accurate attack by well controlled breath on the vibrating vocal folds. The tone resulting from the vocalized breath passing out through the resonators has to be extended and given flexibility.

See page 82.

EXERCISES FOR THE SPEECH ORGANS

THE JAW

This must be free of tenseness and should open widely enough for the voice to pass out freely. It is the lower jaw that moves. It closes by muscular contraction; when this contraction ceases the jaw drops open. Easy effortless dropping is the required image although in fact the action is forward and out. Over-opening weakens tone. Pulling the jaw down and in is a serious fault.

These exercises must be watched in a mirror.

1. Smooth the jaw gently beginning from the hinged joints on either side and passing the fingers lightly down the cheeks to the chin. Do this slowly and induce a feeling of ease as the jaw falls open.

Running the fingers into the hair-line and massaging and loosening the skin over the temples can be a help. Care should be taken to see that back neck muscles are not over-contracted.

2. The second exercise is for agility. The lower jaw moves up and down slowly and easily. Rate is gradually increased until the movement is rapid. Ease is essential.

3. Chewing is the final exercise. This can be either real or imaginary. Both should be done with the lips open and the tongue working vigorously. Chewing a hard apple or a crisp carrot is very good for bringing blood into the gums and for making the jaw flexible.

The Lips

The labial muscle is circular and when it contracts the lips are made into a small circle. The size of this circle can be regulated. Other muscles make it possible to turn the upper lip up and the lower lip down. The lower lip offers little difficulty but exercises may be needed to make the upper lip flexible. A stiff upper lip is an enemy to good voice and speech. If the sides of the lips are drawn-back the tone is thinned and articulation made more difficult.

4. Look in a mirror and ease the lips. Let them lie softly together.

5. Turn the upper lip up; turn it back on itself. Help it with the finger if it refuses to move. Hold a pencil in the upper lip.

6. Stroke the sides of the lips forward bringing about a pouting position.

7. Press the lips together flattening them into African 'plate' position.

8. Practise the various lip positions: neutral, open lip-rounding, and close lip-rounding. (See 'Lip-shaping' under 'Vowel Sounds', page 56).

The Tongue

The flexibility of the tongue has to be ensured by making it as economical and accurate in its movement as possible. Besides playing a part in the production of tone the tongue does much of the work of articulation.

9. Thrust the tongue out of the mouth into a sharp point making sure it does not go downhill but juts levelly from the mouth. It may help to hold a finger in front of the mouth and try to point the tongue to its top. When the tongue is withdrawn into the mouth its tip should contact the backs of the lower teeth. Repeat this exercise slowly, making sure the movement is accurate and gradually increase the speed of it. Accuracy is essential in tongue exercises. (Note: a few people possessing a short frenum may find these exercises cause soreness in which case they should not be done.)

10. Protrude the tongue into a point; raise the pointed tongue as high as possible and lower to as low a position as possible. Do not strain the tongue but do not be afraid of stretching

it. Swing the tongue up and down several times.

11. Put out the tongue and point it. Then swing it to right and then to left as far as possible. Try to acquire the sensation of the swing and stretch of the tongue.

12. Put out the tongue and point it. Let the tongue spread out sideways. Then point it hard again. Alternate these positions rhythmically.

13. Whirl the tongue round in a rhythmical movement.

14. Take an ice-cream cone or an ice lolly and holding it as far away from the mouth as the tongue can reach at a stretch, lick with the tongue in an upward, downward and circular movement. The ice cream is the reward but make sure the tongue works hard to gain it.

15. Close the lips but keep the jaw dropped. Move the tip of the tongue up to the teeth-ridge and down to the backs of the lower teeth. Increase the speed of the movement making sure it is accurate. Open the lips and repeat the exercise.

16. Keep the tip of the tongue contacting the backs of the lower teeth and raise the front to the H*EE*D vowel position. Lower the tongue to the H*AR*D position. Alternate these positions rapidly and accurately.

17. Keep the tip of the tongue contacting the backs of the lower teeth and raise the back of the tongue to a *k* position, then lower it to H*AR*D.

Alternate these positions rapidly.

18. Beginning with the tip of

the tongue contacting the backs of the lower teeth raise the tip and tap the teeth-ridge with it. Do this as rapidly as possible.

The Soft Palate (Velum)

The is a difficult speech organ to exercise and it is difficult to watch. A small torch shone into the mouth facilitates this.

19. Yawn.

20. Keeping the mouth open breathe in through the nose and out through the mouth. Repeat this exercise watching the soft palate rise and fall.

21. Make a H*AR*D sound and then drop the soft palate so that the sound is nasalized and much of the breath passes out through the nose.

When these muscular exercises for the speech organs have been done awareness of the sensation of each organ should be increased.

EXERCISES TO INCREASE KINÆSTHETIC SENSORY AWARENESS OF THE SPEECH ORGANS

The Lips

1. Dampen the lips slightly. Put them together gently and hum quietly making the lips tingle. Then increase the power of the hum.

2. 'Bumble' on the lips. Make a *b* sound in an easy bumbly way and repeat it. Aim at sounding like a bass drum. Explode *b* into *m*.

3. Blow out through the lips making them roll. Do this up and down the scale.

THE TONGUE

4. Hum on an *n* sound connecting the nasal sensation with that between the tip of the tongue and the teeth-ridge.

5. Repeat *d* rapidly but avoid slurring it. Explode *d* into *n*.

6. Roll *r* on the tip of the tongue and sing it up and down the scale. It is a good test of breath control if the downwards scale can be sustained.

THE SOFT PALATE

7. Hum on *ng* varying the pitch. Add clicks (tut-tut etc.).

8. Repeat *g* rapidly, aiming at full voicing.

9. Roll an *r* sound between the uvula and the back of the tongue.

ORGANS INTER-ACTING

10. Make tip of tongue *r*, bring in a lip-roll, add a uvular *r*. Keep all three going.

11. Say BIFFITTO-DAD-DIKER changing rhythm, pitch and volume. Move as you do this. Repeat with ZIN-NIPU-JOCKERWOF.

THE PURPOSE OF THE RESONATOR SCALE IN TONE EXERCISES

After the speech organs have been exercised separately the next step is to combine the speech organs to form a complete resonator. Each speech organ being flexible and controlled can maintain its position as part of the mouth resonator. This sustained position forms a pure vowel sound and the various positions of the resonator scale are identified by taking the name of the nearest vowel. The two vowel glides included in the resonator scale (H*OE* and H*AY*) have to be practised as pure vowels. This does NOT mean that they lose their quality in speech where they should of course be glides.

As an introduction to the resonator scale a shortened version of it is used. This employs the five main sounds and arranges them thus:

FIGURE-OF-EIGHT

H*AY* H*AW*K

H*EE*D H*AR*D H*OOT*

H*AY* H*AW*K

This arrangement begins with H*AR*D which is a convenient starting point because for this vowel the tongue is low in the mouth.

The principle is that the speech organs assume the position of the vowel and then the outgoing breath is passed steadily through it so that the Resonant Pitch is heard. (Resonant pitch is heard only when unvocalized breath is passed through the resonators. Resonant pitch should not be confused with vocal pitch.)

The breath must pass out with good direction from the diaphragm; it should be a gentle, full outpouring, free from any rasping sound, with the resonant pitch audible only if the listener's ear is brought near the mouth. The ribs are kept extended and the sensation of controlling the breath from the diaphragm links up with the sensation of the breath passing out without restriction but through a steadily held position.

Certain points should be remembered in addition to those already described:

1. The learning phase is difficult and should be taken slowly and carefully.

2. The vowel position must be accurate and free from tension. The tongue tip contacts the backs of the lower teeth.
3. The jaw has to be comfortably but sufficiently open. The width depends upon the size of the individual mouth. For the opening measured between the front teeth $\frac{3}{8}$ of an inch is frequently sufficient; some people need more. The open-jaw position must be kept as the speech organs move from position to position. The changes must not be made by jaw movement.
4. There should be a renewal of breath between each vowel position. A clean attack on the new position is needed.

The figure-of-eight sequence moves from
H*AR*D to H*AY*.

H*AY* is formed by raising the front of the tongue towards the hard palate. The next position is the close vowel

H*EE*D. When this is made care must be taken not to tense the tongue and so produce a hard sound. Protruding the tongue is another fault.

After H*EE*D the tongue lowers again and passes through H*AY* returning to H*AR*D.

The back of the tongue then comes into play. It is essential to be aware of its rising action if the back vowels are to be accurately formed. If the rising action of the back of the tongue is understood due care can be taken to keep the muscular action free. In the second arm of the figure-of-eight the BACK of the tongue rises and the lips round. The half-way position is

H*AW*K.

To make this sound the back of the tongue is raised nearly half-way towards the soft palate and the lips are in open lip-rounded position (see page 57). Finally, the back of the tongue rises to a close position and the lips move to a close lip-rounded position and the vowel produced is

H*OO*T.

The figure-of-eight returns to H*AW*K and back to H*AR*D.

When the sequence has been practised by breathing through it, it should be vocalized.

The attack of the breath on the vowel position is of vital importance. A common fault during such practice is a hard vocal attack. This can be prevented by placing *h* before the vowel. This *h* can be retained mentally until good attack becomes a habit. Work on the resonator scale sequence not only ensures good tone, as the resonators are used fully and in co-operation with good breath control, but also enables the vowel positions to be learned and practised. Accuracy should be the aid of vowel positioning. The change from one position to another should be done with as much economy as possible.

When the resonant pitch is correct, well attacked and sustained, the next stage is to pass vocalized breath through the positioned resonators and so make TONE. The vibrating air-stream will receive one quality as it passes through the neck and another as it passes through the mouth. When the vowel position has a different resonant pitch in the mouth from the neck (H*AR*D to H*EE*D) the double quality is distinguishable. It is particularly easy to hear in H*EE*D.

The neck gives warm supporting quality to tone and this is LOWER RESONANCE; it gives the voice 'body'. It is easily heard in high voices and gives the backing to the tone which prevents a high voice being thin and reedy.

TONE EXERCISES

1. Work on the figure-of-eight on the principle already described in detail above.
2. Extend these exercises to the full resonator-scale sequence. *These achieve balanced tone resulting from a well directed breath force passing through correctly positioned resonators.*
3. Humming on *m*. This begins quietly humming into cupped hands. The mask of the face should 'come alive'. An illusion of humming well outside the mouth gives the breath strength and direction.
4. Humming on *n* concentrating on a buzzing through the nose.
5. Humming on *ng*. The naso-pharynx responds to this and the inside of the head has a vibrating sensation.
6. The resonator scale sequence can be combined with the nasal sounds in the following ways:

(*a*) in initial positions,
(*b*) in final positions,
(*c*) initially and finally,
(*d*) in an inter-vowel position (or 'medial' position).

7. Any consonants can be combined with the vowel sequence for practice. Particularly valuable ones for tone are:

   b d g v *TH*EN z MEA*S*URE w y

8. Sung scales are a vital part of voice training and should be done to a descant recorder or guitar. Such scales are valuable in training pitch; they extend the range and flexibility of the speaking voice. (See page 85(6)).

At this point exercises for tone merge into vocal application and further ones are given on page 82.

COMMON FAULTS OF TONE

1. It is possible to have too much lower resonance. The effect of this is a 'booming' undertone. It is a sign of inexpert voice training.
2. Another common fault is for the voice to be over-resonant. This again is a fault due to poor training. The effect is of 'noise'. Clarity is marred and flexibility impeded as well as the voice being difficult to listen to.
3. Hard vocal attack has already been described and is often a sign of general tenseness which makes the tone thin and hard.
4. Insufficient breath can harden tone because, instead of the diaphragm controlling adequate outgoing breath, the upper chest is tensed to drive out the breath with sufficient force to make phonation possible.
5. Weak faltering tone is another fault due to inadequate breath.
6. When the balance of resonance is considered the nose as well as the mouth and neck plays a vital part. This part is more obvious when the nose is not in a healthy state.

   In English, except for the nasal sounds *m*, *n* and *ng*, the soft palate is raised towards the back wall of the pharynx and this considerably reduces the amount of breath passing out through the nose. When it is raised towards the wall of the pharynx there is space for some breath to pass out through the nose giving direct resonance, but a vital part is played by sympathetic resonance (see page 32).

There are many faults covered by the term 'nasal tone'. If the soft palate is insufficiently raised, too much breath passes out through the nose and the tone is excessively nasal. This is a HYPER-RHINO condition (*hyper*, over-much; *rhino*, nose). When the nasal passage is blocked and no breath passes out through it the tone again sounds nasal and and this a HYPO-RHINO condition (*hypo*, under; *rhino*, nose). The terms are unimportant except for supplying a convenient label for these forms of nasality. Partial blockage may be due to a deviated septum (out-of-line middle nose bone.) There is also PSEUDO-NASALITY and its effect sounds very like the others; this is caused by muscular tenseness in the area of the larynx.

PART IV: WORD

SUMMARY

The general function of the resonators is to produce tone; their particular function is to produce speech sounds. This is done by particular parts of the oral resonator known as speech organs. Vowels are made by vocalized breath passing freely through the mouth and the speech organs positioning to impose a particular shape on it. Consonants are made by the speech organs positioning to impede the passage of the outgoing breath. Vowels and consonants group together to form words. Sounds cannot be made without air being set in motion. We speak of the pulmonic egressive air-stream (pulmonic, from the lungs; egressive, outgoing; air-stream, note that it is moving).

THE SPEECH ORGANS

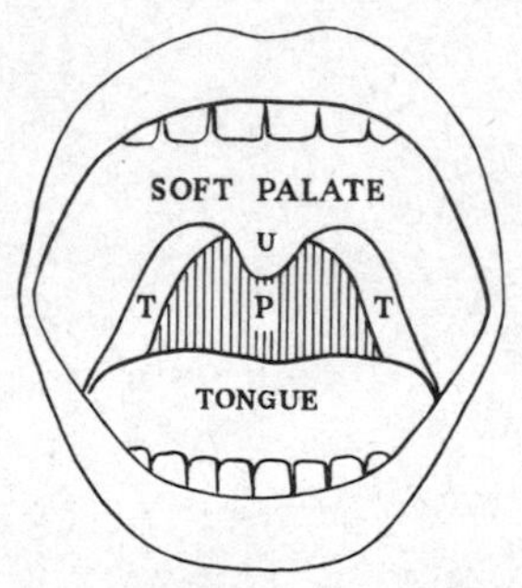

View of the inside of the mouth seen from the front
U, Uvula; *T*, Tonsils (if present); *P*, Pharynx

Working from the lips inwards the speech organs are:

Lips

These are the free edges of the mouth. They are opened by dropping the jaw. There is a muscle running round the lips and by its contraction the lips move and make the lip positions required for some speech sounds.

Look in a mirror and study each speech organ observing its various movements. Connect the speech sounds with parts of the mouth.

Jaw

The lower jaw bone is attached to the facial bones by hinge joints. It is in an open position for most speech sounds.

Observe the jaw positions when the following sounds are made
s f H*AR*D

Teeth

These are attached in curved rows to the upper and lower jaws. The upper front teeth, the incisors and canines, overlap the lower jaw teeth.

Observe your own tooth formation and the way in which breath is affected by them during the formation of *f v f*ast *v*ast *th th*in *th*en.

Teeth-Ridge (or Alveolar Ridge)

This is the ridge between the upper teeth and the curving hard palate.

Several consonants are articulated against this ridge. Feel it with the tongue-tip and practise *t d n r l.*

Hard Palate

This forms the roof of the mouth and separates it from the nasal cavity. Its foundation is a horizontal bone arch.

Study this arch in the mirror and trace it with the tongue-tip.

Soft Palate

The hard palate forms two-thirds of the whole palate. The back third is the soft palate. It continues from the hard palate and is arched. Its back edge is free and from the middle of it there is a projection called the Uvula. The tonsils are embedded in it, one on each side of the uvula.

Drop the jaw and breathe in through the mouth and out through the nose keeping the mouth open. The movement of the soft palate will be seen.

The back part of the soft palate can move freely. Another term for the soft palate is the VELUM.

TONGUE

This lies on the floor of the mouth and turns at a right angle to form part of the front wall of the pharynx. The mouth part of the tongue is free and the tip and sides touch the teeth. The tongue is largely formed of muscle and so is very mobile. Underneath the tongue attaching it to the floor of the mouth is a ligament called the FRENUM.

Parts of the tongue (these do not correspond to any anatomical features but are convenient divisions for the classification of speech sounds):

TIP: the point of the tongue.

BLADE: the part underneath the upper teeth-ridge when the tongue is at rest.

FRONT: this lies under the hard palate.

CENTRE: this lies partly under the hard palate and partly under the soft.

BACK: the part underneath the soft palate.

These are the parts of the tongue concerned with speech. They lie in the mouth and make up the part that can be seen when the mouth is opened.

ROOT: this lies in the throat.

Study your own tongue and identify the parts.

VOCAL FOLDS (OR VOCAL CORDS).

These are a pair of free edges running from front to back across the larynx. The space between them is the glottis.

Besides vibrating and so vocalizing the breath the vocal folds are also a speech organ. The plosive sound made by them in the same way as the lips make *p* is not a recognized sound in English although it is used extensively. The fricative consonant *h* is the friction produced as breath passes through the narrowed glottis.

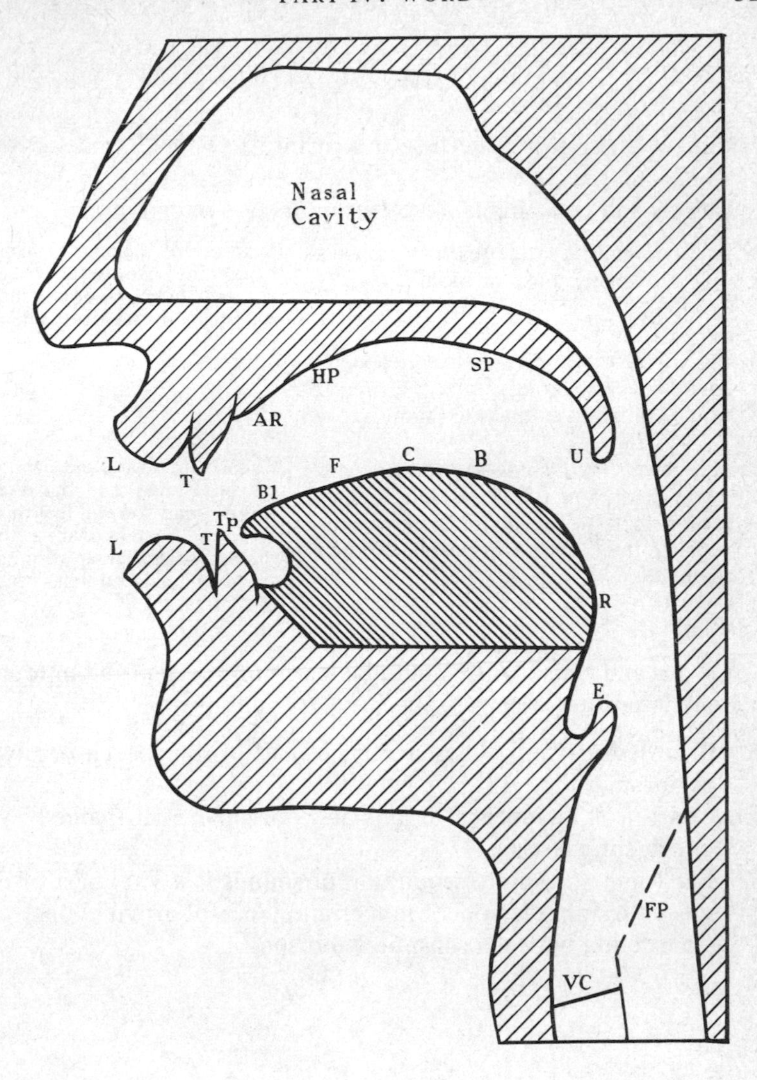

Diagrammatic view of a section through nose, mouth and neck showing the parts of the mouth used in describing speech sounds

L, Lips; *T*, Teeth; *AR*, Alveolar Ridge; *HP*, Hard Palate; *SP*, Soft Palate; *U*, Uvula; *VC*, Vocal folds or cords; *FP*, Food Passage

Tongue: *Tp*, Tip; *Bl*, Blade; *F*, Front; *C*, Centre; *B*, Back; *R*, Root

The Soft Palate is shown in the lowered position

SPEECH SOUNDS

The main division of speech sounds is into VOWELS and CONSONANTS.

Vowels and consonants have certain factors in common:

1. Both are made by the breath as it passes out through the nose or mouth.

   Be aware of the sensation of the breath. Learn to recognize the formation of vowels and consonants by 'feeling' them.

2. Individual differences between speech sounds depend largely upon the speech organs involved in making them.

3. All vowels and some consonants are made with VOCALIZED BREATH. This means that the vocal folds vibrate or vocalize the breath as it passes through them.

   If you place your hand lightly on your throat and make a voiced sound you will feel this vibration. When in doubt as to whether sound in a word is voiced or unvoiced make this test.

Vowels and consonants should be learnt and recognized in four equally important ways:

1. Knowledge of how they are made and of the speech organs performing the task.
2. Control of the speech organs and muscular skill (gained by intelligent exercising).
3. Ear training. Aural recognition of sounds is a vital part of a speech training lesson. (Manner and place of articulation.)
4. Connection between sensation and speech.

VOWELS (VOCOIDS)

A Vowel is made by vocalized breath passing through the mouth. The individual quality of each Vowel is imposed by the positioning of the speech organs.

Vowels divide into
(*a*) PURE VOWELS and
(*b*) VOWEL GLIDES (DIPHTHONGS)

PURE VOWELS

During the formation of these vowels the speech organs are held in one position.

The tongue is mainly responsible for the formation of vowels. The principal factor in determining the nature of a vowel is the part of the tongue which is raised and the height to which it is raised.

For purposes of classification of vowels the tongue is divided into

FRONT

CENTRE

BACK

If the tongue is raised near to the roof of the mouth it is a CLOSE position. If the tongue is low it is an OPEN position.

Two points should be remembered when vowels are practised:

1. The jaw should be open and easy.
2. The tip of the tongue should contact the backs of the lower front teeth.

Always practise vowel shaping with a mirror. Look in it and check the positions.

A good vowel sound depends upon:

1. An accurate positioning of the speech organs.
2. A steadily held position.
3. A steady breath stream.

Put a clean spoon on the front of your tongue and say the vowels

H*A*D and H*EE*D.

The first is low and the second high.

FRONT OF TONGUE VOWELS

Drop the jaw and make sure the tip of the tongue is contacting the backs of the lower teeth.

The FRONT of the tongue is the part lying under the hard palate. Watch this part of the tongue and make the lowest most open English front vowel
H*A*D.
Pass on to the next one which is a little higher in position
H*EA*D.
Then say
H*I*D.
and finally
H*EE*D.
H*I*D and H*EE*D will be seen to be close vowels with the tongue raised near the palate. For H*EE*D it is very close.

From this an arrangement of these vowels can be made:

FRONT OF TONGUE

H*EE*D (CLOSE) Tongue high in the mouth.

H*I*D

H*EA*D

H*A*D (OPEN) Tongue low in the mouth.

BACK OF TONGUE VOWELS

These are difficult to observe because they have a lip articulation as well as the tongue position. When these vowels are practised during speech lessons the accuracy of the sound is achieved by the ear and attention is concentrated on the lip position. A clean finger placed on the back of the tongue will enable the rise of the back of the tongue to be felt. The BACK of the tongue is the part underneath the soft palate.

Beginning with the back of the tongue low in the mouth make the vowel

H*A*RD.

This vowel and the vowel H*U*T are often regarded as back of tongue vowels but in fact they are made with the centre of the tongue today. They are shown in a centralized position on the chart.

Follow with the vowels H*O*CK and H*AW*K. For this sequence the back of the tongue rises slightly. H*U*T is about on a height with H*AW*K and its central position has already been considered.

The last two back vowels are close and so the tongue is high when they are made. They are H*OO*K and H*OO*T.

The back of the tongue vowels can be arranged thus:

	BACK OF TONGUE	
	H*OO*T	TONGUE HIGH IN MOUTH
	H*OO*K	(CLOSE VOWEL POSITION)
		$\frac{1}{2}$-CLOSE
	H*AW*K	
		$\frac{1}{2}$-OPEN
H*U*T		TONGUE LOW IN MOUTH
	H*O*CK	
H*A*RD		(OPEN VOWEL POSITION)

Vowels are identified according to the part of the tongue making them, Front, Centre and Back, and the height of that part, Open, Close, and equally spaced between these, $\frac{1}{2}$-Open and $\frac{1}{2}$-Close.

For example: H*EE*D is a long relatively pure Close Front Vowel (relatively pure: see page 58, under 'Long Vowels'), and H*U*T is a Short Pure $\frac{1}{2}$-Open Central Vowel.

Practise the front vowels from H*A*D to H*EE*D and watch the front of the tongue rising (keep the tip low). Practise the back vowels from H*AR*D to H*OO*T, remembering that most of them also have a lip-shaping.

Front, centre and back vowels can be put together to form a plan of pure vowels.

	Front of Tongue	*Centre of Tongue*	*Back of Tongue*
CLOSE	H*EE*D		H*OO*T
	H*I*D		H*OO*K
$\frac{1}{2}$-CLOSE		H*EA*RD	
	H*EA*D	*A*BOUT	H*AW*K
$\frac{1}{2}$-OPEN		H*U*T	
	H*A*D		H*O*CK
OPEN		H*AR*D	

H*OO*T is a back-vowel that has recently moved a little towards centre.
H*OO*K and H*I*D are positioned considerably towards centre

LIP-SHAPING

The lip-shaping which several back vowels have is vital to their formation. It is possible to make a clearly recognizable vowel sound without lip-rounding by compensating for the absence of this by means of a different tongue position. The lip and tongue positions as described are however recommended in order to achieve the best result.

NEUTRAL LIP POSITION

Most vowels have a neutral lip position. Vowels should be practised with a comfortable jaw opening probably rather less than $\frac{1}{2}$ inch.

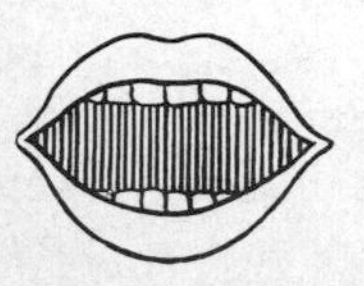

This illustration shows the lips in a neutral position with a medium jaw opening likely to be used in vigorous speech.

OPEN LIP ROUNDING

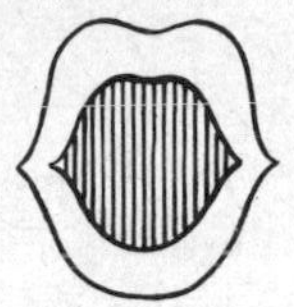

One vowel has open lip rounding. It is H*O*CK. The jaw position shown is an open one. Vowels with bi-labial secondary articulation (some degree of lip-rounding) demonstrate the lip positioning when said in isolation. In connected speech very little lip rounding occurs. The tongue position compensates for it.

MEDIUM LIP ROUNDING

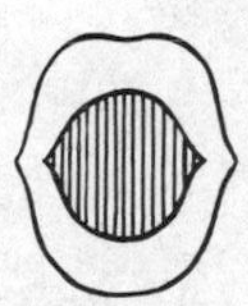

Two vowels have medium lip rounding. These are H*OO*K and H*AW*K. The illustration shows an open jaw position.

CLOSE LIP ROUNDING

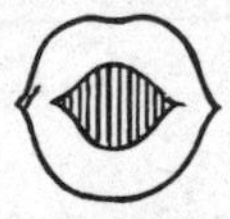

This shows the close lip rounding used for the vowel H*OO*T.

When these vowels are either the starting point or the finishing point of a vowel glide the appropriate degree of lip rounding is used.

Vowel Length

The length of a vowel (the length of time it is sustained) depends on its position in the word. Luckily if English is one's mother tongue this does not have to be consciously learnt and applied.

In the following list the length shortens:

H*E* (Very long in this open position.)
H*EE*D (The vowel shortens when followed by a consonant.)

H*EA*T (A consonant without voice shortens it yet more.)
H*EA*TING (The vowel is shorter still when another syllable follows.)

Knowledge of vowel length is important to avoid undue lengthening of vowels in an effort to clarify or improve speech. If vowels are given undue length the balance of enunciation is upset and the speech sounds unnatural. However in spite of these slight variations vowels are intrinsically long or short because they are easier to say that way.

LONG VOWELS

These include all vowel glides and the following pure vowels:

H*EE*D
H*EAR*D
H*AR*D
H*AW*K
H*OO*T

You may be aware of a slight glide when you say H*EE*D and H*OO*T. They are pure vowels but are only relatively so. The glide is not long enough for them to be classed as vowel glides.

SHORT VOWELS

H*I*D
H*EA*D
H*A*D
*A*BOUT
H*U*T
H*O*CK
H*OO*K

The Effect of Emphasis and Word Stress on Vowel Length

The relationships of vowel length already described apply when vowels are compared in identical circumstances. Emphasis placed on a word will tend to lengthen the vowel in that word (or stressed syllable of that word) though it remains a short vowel.

Many people would considerably lengthen the short vowel in the word 'bad' when stressing the word in a phrase such as 'It's thoroughly b*a*d'.

Conversely a long vowel in an unstressed syllable may be shortened although it remains a long vowel.

Compare the length of the vowel in the first syllable of 'August' (month of the year) in which this vowel receives word stress with the length of this vowel in the word 'august' (adjective) in which the word stress is on the second syllable.

VOWEL GLIDES

The speech organs making a vowel glide move throughout its formation. It may be defined as

A continuous glide from one vowel position towards a second.

There are eight English vowel glides. All are falling glides: this means that the weight comes at the beginning of the glide.

The eight divide into

THREE CENTRING VOWEL GLIDES and

FIVE CLOSING VOWEL GLIDES

CENTRING VOWEL GLIDES

To make these glides the speech organs begin in a front or back vowel position and glide towards the central vowel *A*BOUT.

H*ERE* begins at H*I*D and glides towards *A*BOUT.

H*ARE* begins at H*EA*D (said with a low tongue position) and glides towards *A*BOUT.

T*OUR* begins at H*OO*K and glides towards *A*BOUT.

CLOSING VOWEL GLIDES

To make these glides the tongue rises in the mouth. It moves from one vowel position to a second which is closer (or nearer) to the roof of the mouth.

H*AY* begins at H*EA*D and glides towards H*I*D.

(This is a short glide made by the front of the tongue.)

H*IGH* begins at an open (low) front tongue position and glides towards H*I*D.

(This is a long glide made by the front of the tongue.)

H*OW* begins at an open (low) central tongue position and glides towards H*OO*K.

(This is a long glide passing from an open central position towards a fairly close back one.)

H*OY* begins at H*O*CK said with a low tongue position and glides towards H*I*D.

(This is a long glide from a fairly open back position through the centre tongue towards a front fairly close position.)

H*OE* begins at a fairly close (high) central position and glides towards H*OO*K.

(This is a short glide made from the centre of the tongue towards a closer back position.)

In T*OUR*, H*OW*, H*OY* and H*OE* vowels are involved which have lip rounding and the appropriate degree should be used when making the glide.

Remember all vowels are practised with a low tip of tongue position. Maintain this position when practising vowel glides.

Avoid making two sounds when practising these. The aim should be a gradual and continuous movement of the speech organs concerned and the result a glide.

Additional Vowel Glides

H*OAR* begins at H*AW*K and glides towards *A*BOUT.

This is used by some speakers in words such as 'four' 'bore' 'door' instead of H*AW*K.

F*IRE* begins with the front of the tongue even lower than the H*A*D position and glides towards *A*BOUT.

This glide is more likely to be used in words such as 'wire' 'pyre' than the two-syllabled pronunciation W + H*IGH* + *A*BOUT.

FL*OWER* begins at H*AR*D and glides towards *A*BOUT.

Many speakers use this in words such as 'power' 'shower' instead of the two-syllabled p + H*OW* + *A*BOUT.

CONSONANTS (CONTOIDS)

Whereas a vowel must have a free passage through the mouth a consonant is made by the outgoing breath being impeded in some way. These ways are various and the nature of several of them can be guessed from their names.

A PLOSIVE is connected with an explosion.

A NASAL obviously must be a sound made through the nose.

LATERAL (or sideways) can refer to only one sound in English (*l*).

A FRICATIVE must be sound with friction in it.

Some consonants are made with unvocalized breath and some with vocalized breath. All consonants are made with the velum raised, except the nasals (in the formation of which the breath goes out through the nose).

Consonants made with vocalized breath are known as VOICED.

Consonants not made with vocalized breath are known as VOICELESS.

Voiced consonants are made with weaker breath pressure than the voiceless counterparts.

Here is a list of ways in which the breath escapes and the resultant sounds:

PLOSIVE CONSONANTS

These are made by a total blockage of the air passage through the mouth by contact between two speech organs. Breath pressure increases behind the contact (this is called the HOLD or STOP) and an explosion is heard when the organs part.

p *b*
t *d*
k *g*

AFFRICATE CONSONANTS (APPROXIMANTS)

These begin in the same way as plosives with the contact and hold of two speech organs. Instead of a quick clean release there is a gradual release and friction is

*ch*in *g*in
or *ch*eer *j*eer

heard as the organs part. An affricate is one sound.

NASAL CONSONANTS

In making these the mouth passage is completely blocked by the contact of two speech organs and the soft palate lowers so that all the air passes out through the nose resulting in a nasal sound.

m
n
si*ng*

LATERAL CONSONANTS

When the middle of the outgoing air passage is blocked (by raising the tongue to contact the teeth-ridge but keeping the sides lowered) the breath escapes sideways or laterally.

*l*ane
fu*ll*

ROLLED AND FLAPPED CONSONANTS

A flapped consonant is made by the contact and release of two speech organs (there is little build-up of air pressure as with a plosive). A rolled consonant is two or more flaps repeated. A flapped consonant has one tap only. Flapped *r* is made by the tongue tapping once at the back of the teeth-ridge.

spi*r*it
powe*r* of

FRICATIVE CONSONANTS

Friction is heard when two speech organs are very close together so narrowing the passage of the outgoing breath.

*th*in	*th*en
f	*v*
s	*z*
*s*ure	mea*s*ure
h	
	r

SEMI-VOWELS

These begin in the position of very close vowels and the sound consists of a rapid

w
y

movement (or glide) towards another vowel. They are classed as consonants because they function as such.

The Organs Making Consonants

When the nature of consonant sounds has been grasped the question of which organs make them has to be considered.

Labial to do with the lips.
Bi-Labial to do with both lips.
Dental to do with the teeth.
Alveolar to do with the teeth-ridge (alveolar ridge).
Lingual to do with the tongue.
Velar to do with the soft palate (velum).
Palatal to do with the hard palate.
Glottal to do with the vocal folds (the glottis is the space between the vocal folds).

A simple chart can be made, as shown below.

CONSONANT CHART

	Bi-labial	Labio-dental	Dental	Alveolar	Palato-alveolar	Palatal	Velar	Glottal
Plosives	*p* *b*			*t* *d*			*k* *g*	
Affricates					*ch*in *g*in			
Nasals	*m*			*n*			si*ng*	
Laterals				*l*ane fu*ll*				
Fricatives		*f* *v*	*th*in *th*en	*s* *z* *r*	*s*ure mea*s*ure			*h*
Flapped				*r*				
Semi-Vowels	*w*					*y*et		

DETAILS OF THE CONSONANTS

TO MAKE:

p the lips come together; breath pressure increases whilst they are together; when they part an explosive sound is heard.

b the process is the same as for *p* but the breath force is weaker and the sound is voiced, as the vibrating vocal folds vocalize the outgoing breath.

Remember it takes time to learn to know and recognize sounds.

The plosives have three parts: APPROACH as the organs come into contact; HOLD, they remain together as breath pressure builds up; RELEASE as they part and the breath escapes and the plosive is completed. Be aware of these parts.

t the tip of the tongue rises and touches the teeth-ridge; breath pressure increases during this contact; an explosive sound is heard when the tip of the tongue is quickly removed.

The teeth-ridge can be felt. It is the clearly marked rather bumpy ridge behind the upper teeth.

d the process is the same as for *t* but the breath force is weaker and it is voiced.

In whispered speech it is the weaker breath pressure of voiced consonants that enables them to be distinguished from their voiceless counterparts.

k is made by the back of the tongue rising to contact the raised soft palate; breath pressure increases during the contact; when the tongue lowers an explosive sound is heard.

The soft palate is the soft movable part of the roof of the mouth behind the hard palate. It can be felt with the tongue.

g the process is the same as for *k* but the breath pressure is weaker and it is voiced.

*ch*in is made by the tip of the tongue rising and making contact just behind the teeth-ridge; the breath pressure increases during the tip-of-tongue contact; instead of a quick clean release being made the tip of the tongue comes away slowly and friction is heard.

gin is made in the same way as *ch*in except that it is voiced.

This slow release of a plosive resulting in the addition of a fricative consonant is known as AFFRICATION. With *t* and *d* it makes the affricates *ch*in and gin but slow release of others is a fault. (See page 81 Fricatives (*a*)) m is made by the lips coming together so that there is no way out for the breath except through the nose. The soft palate is lowered to let this happen. It is a voiced sound.

If you make an *m* and then take all the voice out of it you will feel a strong current of air passing down the nose.

n is made in the same way as *m* except that the mouth opening is closed by the tip of the tongue rising and contacting the teeth-ridge with the sides contacting the molars.

si*ng* is made in the same way as *m* except that the mouth opening is cut off by the contact of the back of the tongue which is raised to the soft palate which is lowered.

*l*ane is made by the tip of the tongue rising and contacting the teeth-ridge; the sides of the tongue are in a lowered position; the breath escapes from the mouth by going round the middle obstruction made by the tongue. Consequently the breath escapes sideways or laterally. It is a voiced sound. In clear *l* the front of the tongue is raised towards the hard palate giving a 'vowel resonance' similar to H*I*D.

This sideways escape can be plainly felt if the voice is taken out of the sound.
l before a vowel is a CLEAR *l*.

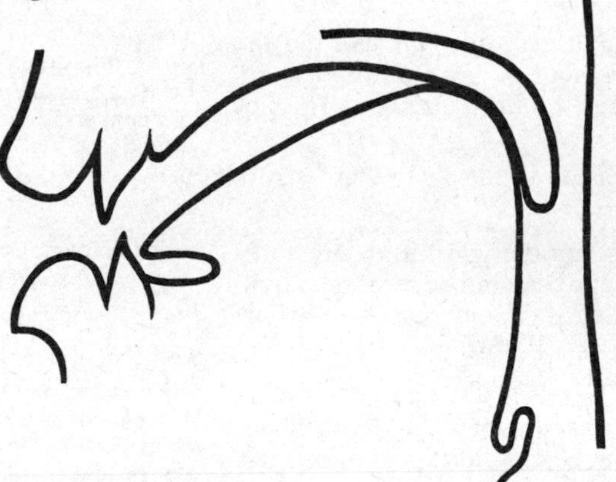

Diagram showing the position of the tongue and soft palate during the formation of 'SI*NG*'
Sagittal section through the median line of the tongue

ful*l* is made in the same way as clear *l* except that the front of the tongue is low and the back is raised towards the soft palate giving a quality reminiscent of the vowel in H*OO*K.

This is DARK *l* and is used in a final position and before a consonant.

*th*in is made by the tip of the tongue being placed against the backs of the teeth; friction is heard as the breath passes through the spaces.

*th*en is made in the same way as *th*in, except that it is voiced.

f is the audible friction heard when the upper teeth and the lower lip touch and breath is forced out between the spaces.

It is the inside of the lower lip that makes the sound. Don't 'bite' the lip.

v is made in the same way as *f* except that it is voiced.

s is made by the breath being forced through a narrow groove made by the sides of the tongue touching the roof of the mouth leaving a channel down the middle. The blade of the tongue articulates it against the teeth ridge. The tip is high or low.

The friction is made in the narrow gap between the blade of the tongue and the teeth-ridge.

z is made in the same way as *s* but it is voiced.

*s*ure is made in the same way as *s* but the groove is not so narrow and friction occurs over a longer distance. The lips are protruded.

The particularly piercing quality of this sound enables it to be used to penetrate a babble of conversation and secure attention.

mea*s*ure is made in the same way as *s*ure but is voiced.

h is made when the vocal folds are sufficiently approximated to produce audible friction as breath passes between them.

h can be demonstrated by taking the voice out of any vowel.

*r*un is made by raising the tip of the tongue close to just behind the teeth-ridge. During the past twenty years or so *r* has lost most of its friction and is a frictionless continuant. It is a voiced sound and has some lip protrusion.

Fricative *r*, or the frictionless continuant, is used in Received Pronunciation in all positions except that the flapped variety is used by some speakers between vowels.

Examples of the use of flapped *r* are:

pe*r*iod is flapped or 'one-tap' *r* and is made by the tip of the tongue tapping once against the back of the teeth-ridge. It is a voiced sound.

(*a*) within a word; for example, Mary, period, hurry.
(*b*) as LINKING *r* in phrases such as 'far away', 'her age'. Many people find it easier to sound the *r* at the end of a word when the next word begins with a vowel.
When flapped *r* is used it gives the speech extra clarity.

w has its primary articulation made by the lips. A raising of the back of the tongue also takes place as a secondary articulation. Both lips and tongue immediately glide towards the vowel following and it is this glide which makes the sound.

*y*et is made by the front of the tongue rising very close to the hard palate and gliding immediately towards another vowel.

Semi-vowels are very near to being vowels but it is preferable to regard them as consonants because (*a*) they cannot be sustained and (*b*) they behave as consonants in that the preconsonantal form of the indefinite article is used before words beginning with them. For example 'a yard' not 'an yard' and 'a wood' and not 'an wood'.

VOWELS AND CONSONANTS IN CONNECTED SPEECH

So far each sound has been considered as a separate entity. When sounds are linked together to form syllables what is heard is not a series of separate sounds but a series of sounds merging into each other. Between two voiced sounds vocalization continues and as the speech organs move into position to make the second sound a slight speech glide is heard.

In connected speech sounds are rarely given their full value. Slight changes come about because the sound is easier to say if it is slightly modified.

PHONEMIC VARIANTS (ALLOPHONES)

Sounds in a language have slight changes caused by neighbouring sounds. PHONEME is another term for speech sounds as used in this book. Phonemic variants or allophones are modifications made to a sound by the influence of its neighbouring sounds. The slight variations in the sounds keep the word easily recognizable and in no way change the meaning.

As an example some of the phonemic variants of *k* are considered here. Speak the word KEEN and notice the lip position of *k* (neutral). Now say the same sounds with a *w* between *k* and H*EE*D saying the word QUEEN and you will find that the strong lip rounding of *w* makes *k* also lip rounded.

Speak KEEN noticing the place of articulation between the back of the tongue and the soft palate. Now speak COON and you will find the place of articulation has moved back considerably. This is through the influence of the back tongue position of the vowel following the *k* in COON.

Another variant is the amount of aspiration which follows the plosion of *k*.

The aspiration is generally less at the end of a syllable than at the beginning: compare KATE and TAKE.

Frequently when one plosive is followed by another the first of the pair is not exploded. In the phrase LOOK KATE the contact and hold of the first *k* are made, then there is a fresh impetus or push of energy and the hold and release of the second *k* (KATE) is made. This INCOMPLETE PLOSION of a plosive consonant is very common and is not confined to identical consonants. Examples are:

A*C*T
BI*G* POLES
BRIGH*T* DAY
BRIGH*T* STAR

The importance of phonemic variants is not in having detailed knowledge of them but in realizing their existence and in keeping the spoken language natural by not speaking each sound as it is made when pronounced in isolation. Balanced accurate enunciation depends upon the use of the correct phonemic variant. If one's mother tongue is English phonemic variants do not have to be learnt. The effect of using the wrong phonemic variant is either one of regional accent or the result of attempting to make changes in one's speech without good teaching.

Another phonemic variant of *k* is when it is exploded sideways or laterally. This is illustrated in the word BUCKLE. The *k* is exploded sideways through the influence of the lateral *l* sound following.

Lateral Plosion

When a plosive consonant is followed by an *l* sound it is released through the *l* position sideways or laterally.

The lateral plosion can be heard when the sounds are at the beginning of a syllable. This lateral quality is an essential part of the formation of *l* and it influences the preceding plosive.

Say the words PLEASE, CLOVER and experience the sideways explosion of the *p* and *k*.

The lateral plosion is often found more difficult when it forms the second syllable of a word such as BOT*TL*E, BUC*KL*E, PEO*PL*E.

Practise the words BOTTLE, BUCKLE, PEOPLE, and avoid making a vowel between the plosive and the *l*.

Another frequent use of phonemic variants is in

Nasal Plosion

When a plosive consonant is released through the nose instead of the mouth it is said to have a nasal plosion. This happens in words in which the plosive is followed by a nasal consonant made in the same articulatory position.

t is exploded through *n* in words such as BUTTON, WRITTEN. The tongue remains on the teeth-ridge and the breath escapes through the nose when the soft palate lowers to make the *n* sound.

Say the word BUTTON. No vowel sound should be made between the *t* and *n*. Other examples are HIDDEN and GARDEN.

Sometimes in connected speech neighbouring sounds cause the replacement of sounds by new ones not phonemic variants of the original. This is known as

Assimilation

This is the process of replacing a sound in a word by another sound because of the strong influence of a third neighbouring sound near it in the word or sentence. An example will make this clear.

Speak the phrase IN TEN MINUTES. The *n* of TEN often becomes an *m*: TEM MINUTES. *n* and *m* have in common the fact that they are nasals but the bilabial influence of the *m* of MINUTES has influenced the alveolar *n* and made it also bilabial.
Other examples are:
JOHN BROOK might become JOHM BROOK; CAN BE—CAM BE; HAND CARVED—HANG CARVED.

Too much assimilation in speech gives the effect of careless enunciation and is to be avoided. A degree of it is acceptable especially when speech is informal. Assimilation is most likely to occur in more rapid styles of speech.

Not only do sounds vary in connected speech. The position of a sound in a word or sentence can lead to its omission. This process is called

Elision

The question of whether a sound is elided depends on its place in a word and the importance of the word in a sentence. A stressed word is less likely to have elided sounds.

A sound frequently elided is *h*.

In a sentence such as THEY MAY HAVE BEEN the *h* of HAVE is likely to be elided.

Sounds in parts of verbs are apt to be elided.

IT IS LIKELY becomes IT'S LIKELY.
IT HAS NOT HAPPENED becomes
IT HASN'T HAPPENED.

The connecting word AND is an example.

TOWN AND COUNTRY has the *d* of AND elided. Take a paragraph. Read it aloud but do not leave out any sound which you would normally put into the word when pronounced by itself. Then take the same paragraph and read it as you would speak it naturally and mark the sounds you have elided. Use recording apparatus.

Another interesting feature of connected speech is

Gradation

It is possible to have more than one pronunciation of a word occurring in spoken English. Some words have a Strong form which is heard when the word is stressed and a Weak form which is heard when the word is in an unimportant position in a sentence. This use of strong and weak forms of the same word is Gradation.

Gradation adds to the natural flow of language. The words are given their weak form because it is easier to say them that way.

There are different styles of speech varying from the Colloquial to the Formal. As one would expect the latter includes few weak forms but the former has quite a number.

Examples of this are seen in the words THE BOY in which the vowel in THE is *A*BOUT and not H*EE*D.

This happens before words which begin with consonants. If the following word begins with a vowel THE is pronounced with a shortened version of H*EE*D.

Speak the sentence THERE ARE TWO OF THEM and observe the gradation.

THE WORD AND CONNECTED SPEECH

Spoken language relies on PAUSE, STRESS and INTONATION to give it meaning and significance.

PAUSE

In speech a pause is a cessation of sound. Pauses are used in all connected speech to mark the sense; they are oral punctuation. The sense can often be further clarified and enhanced by pauses which are not strictly in line with the grammatical construction of the sentence. A word can be given importance by pausing before and after it, thus isolating it and bringing it into prominence. A pause builds up the suspense and it is useful when climax is being reached or when a strong emotional situation is being interpreted. Pauses should be carefully timed. Overlong pauses can break the sense and the feeling during performance. This is particularly so when an audience is present and its reaction has to be considered as well as the meaning of the words being spoken.

In poetry pause has a special part to play in giving the pattern to verse-form. The end-of-line pause can be a final one with a full stop marking the end of the sentence, or a colon, semicolon or comma marking the end of a phrase. When this happens in a poem it is known as an end-stopped line.

Good poets frequently run their sense from one line into the next without a final pause at the line ending. This run-on line is sometimes called an enjambed line. When this occurs one must convey the effect of the sense spilling over into the next line. A pause is made to mark the ending of the first line. The last word of the line is suspended by intonation and duration in order to point forward to a continuation of the sense into the second line; and then a fresh impetus is given to the first word of the next line.

Length of pause is important in poetry. Stanza pauses which mark the end of a stanza should be longer than the linear or end-of-line pause. The continuity of the stanza must be preserved and over-long pauses should not break it.

Poetry has a balancing pause which is the natural pause within the line. The term CAESURA is sometimes applied to this. A good poetry speaker must use this pause. It gives the lilt and balance to a line and adds considerably to the musical quality, often helping to point the sense. A regularly placed caesural pause can be monotonous and its place in the line is varied in good poetry.

STRESS

Stress is the weight placed on a word when it is spoken to give it emphasis.

WORD STRESS

Luckily those speaking English as their mother tongue learn which syllables to stress when familiar words are pronounced. The stress on new words has to be learnt.

SENTENCE STRESS

Sense depends to a large extent on the stress being placed on the right syllable and on the right word in a sentence. Nouns and verbs are usually stressed most heavily. Adjectives and adverbs are stressed but to a lesser degree. Placing the stress on the wrong word can alter or at least warp the meaning. Stress should be dictated by the syntax of the sentence. Heavy stressing makes speech laboured and over-emphatic. Words should be made emphatic by the way the voice moves on them and not by sheer weight of utterance. This movement of the voice is

INTONATION

Intonation is the word used to refer to the changes of pitch made by the voice when speaking. It is one of the chief means by which a speaker gives exactness and subtlety of meaning.

A word or phrase may be spoken with any of several different possible intonations each of which will generally convey some difference of meaning or attitude. In practice, intonation (variation of PITCH) is usually combined with other factors which give meaning and colour and individuality to speech: these are variations of VOLUME, TONE and RHYTHM. It is neither possible nor desirable to separate intonation from these other factors. Like intonation they are the natural means of communicating active thought and feeling and are used by every speaker whose voice and speech mechanisms are responsive to intention. The process is largely unconscious.

With all the possible combinations of pitch, volume, tone and rhythm it is not surprising that two equally expert speakers will rarely speak a sentence in exactly the same way. Each will interpret it in a slightly different manner according to his outlook and style and obvious differences will be expressed in intonation.

The intonation used by a speaker is closely connected with (and to some extent an expression of) his habitual thoughts and attitudes. Many people through lack of sufficiently vital and varied thought or through lack of vocal freedom use a limited set of intonation patterns both in their spontaneous speech and (usually more noticeably) in their interpretations of written material. Some knowledge of the nature and functions of intonation should help them to become aware of their limitations and to extend the range of meanings they can communicate vocally. However the application to interpretation of consciously-conceived intonation should (if done at all) be done with caution or a mechanical effect will result. If intonation is not the result of an inner awareness and comprehension of some significance in the words being spoken it will be artificial and the listener will recognize it as such.

It is impossible within the compass of this book to give more than a very brief résumé of the basic facts of English intonation. Much investigation into this has been done in recent years and a list of books is contained in the Bibliography. The following points should be considered:

(*a*) There are many differences in terminology as used by different writers which may at first be confusing.
(*b*) The books published are primarily for foreign learners of English and their teachers.
(*c*) The analysis is chiefly concerned with everyday conversational English.

Because of (*b*) and (*c*) students of speech and drama whose

native language is English may find the intonat
limited for the interpretation of drama or poetry
useful basis on which to build but in themselves wou
subtlety.

The Marking of Intonation

Instrumental (and therefore objective) analysis of vocal pitch in the speaking of a sentence will show a wavy line rather like the outline of a hilly landscape with gaps where the voiceless sounds occur.

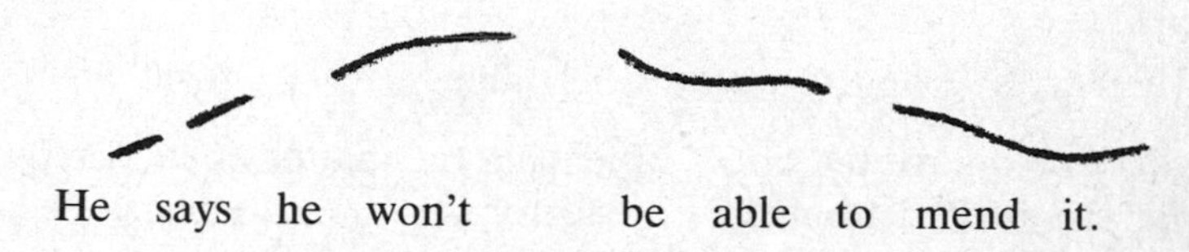

A picture such as that drawn above is not very helpful in practical teaching and intonation marking is usually simplified into a system which is more significant. Several different methods are in use but the simplest to draw makes use of a line for every stressed syllable and a dot for every unstressed syllable. Significant pitch changes nearly always occur on stressed syllables and this is clearly indicated by the direction of the line. Stressed syllables do not always have a pitch change and are frequently spoken on a level pitch which is indicated by a level line. The same sentence as shown above, said with the same intonation, would appear thus:

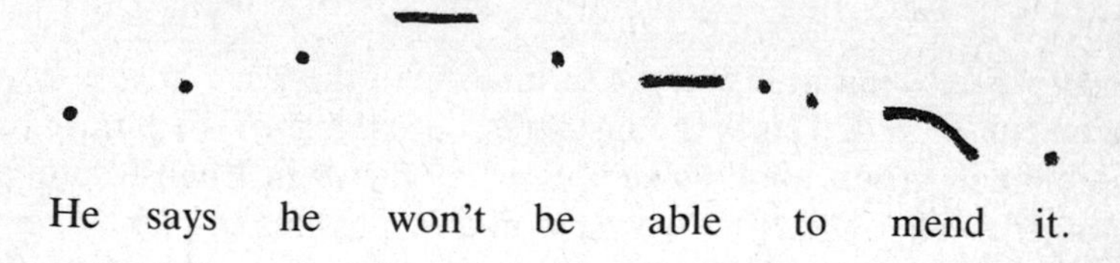

It may be easier to hear an intonation pattern if instead of being spoken it is whistled.

The above falling tune is a basic pattern of unemphatic statement in the English language. A speaker who does not intend to convey special significance will tend to use it. A sequence of sentences said with this tune is bound to be dull since it is merely a series of plain statements unlinked to each other and with no suggestion that there is anything implied but not spoken. On the other hand a refusal to use a falling tune when appropriate is destructive of meaning.

The same sentence said with a rising tune at the end might appear like this:

He says he won't be able to mend it.

This would have the effect of leaving the matter open; a reply perhaps is invited from the listener or an implication has been made which will be understood by the listener. The exact interpretation would depend on the context. No such invitation or implication is usually conveyed by a falling tune which has the inherent quality of finality.

This sentence could also be spoken with a Fall-Rise intonation on the word 'mend'. This might imply that he could not repair it but could provide a replacement.

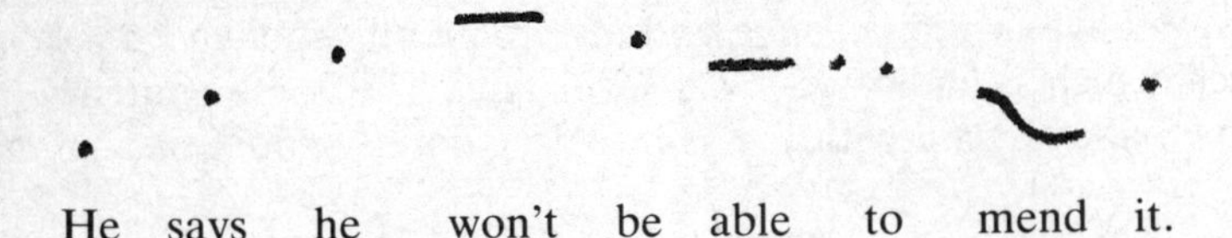

So far only variations on the intonation of the word 'mend' have been considered. This is the last stressed syllable of the phrase (or 'intonation group') and as such is a key factor in English intonation. It is called the NUCLEUS. It would be possible to pick out any of the other words in the sentence by means of intonation (in conjunction with stress) and so give the sentence a different meaning. For example the word 'says' may be given an emphasis by intonation and stress which would imply doubt in the truth of the man's statement that he couldn't mend it. Or the second 'he'

might be emphasised by intonation and stress so as to give the meaning that HE wouldn't be able to mend it but someone else might. And so on.

THE NUCLEUS: This is the most important syllable of an intonation pattern. In words of more than one syllable only the stressed one is kinetic. This one is the NUCLEUS. (Kinetic: the pitch changes throughout its pronunciation.)

Try the following kinetic examples:

			Some possible meanings (depending on context)
1. Low Fall	Yes	╲	Definite affirmative but no enthusiasm. Possibly rather grim.
2. High Fall	Yes	╲	More emphatic; possibly enthusiastic.
3. Low Rise	Yes	╱	Might be said in answering the telephone or casually to your own name or in agreeing with what someone has said so far.
4. High Rise	Yes	╱	Rather surprised or animated.
5. Low Fall-rise	Yes	╲╱	Affirmative with some implication; it could be slight doubt or an invitation to continue.
6. High Fall-Rise	Yes	╲╱	Strong affirmative with an implication; possibly 'I've told you so a dozen times already.'
7. Rise-Fall	Yes	╱╲	Meaning perhaps 'most certainly' or 'I should think so, too!'

Other stressed syllables are:

Level	Yes	—	This hardly exists in English as a complete intonation pattern but only as a part of a larger one nearly always containing a nucleus on which there is a change of pitch. A nearly level low pitch could possibly be used here to indicate utter boredom.

THE HEAD: is the first stressed syllable and the highest pitch of the intonation pattern. See the word WONT in the patterns on pages 75 and 76. Placing the HEAD on the same note again and again is the surest way to be vocally monotonous. Breaking the habit involves pitch training and a monitoring ear.

Patterns are built out of the stressed and intervening unstressed syllables giving intonation that conveys exact meaning and intention. Even when a single word such as the 'Yes' chosen as an illustration is spoken with a certain intonation the exact significance may be so subtle as to defy exact definition in words.

The analysis of intonation is a highly complex subject and the student of speech and drama may well find that his or her own ear and habits aided by the application of a little basic knowledge affords the safest approach. IT IS ESSENTIAL that English speech-tunes be employed and tricks and exaggerations avoided.

WORD AND VOCAL PRACTICE

Exercises for the word fall into two parts. The first is concerned with the formation of individual vowels and consonants by the speech organs. These organs have already been exercised during the work on tone. Vowel shapes have been made accurate during the resonator scale practice. In this section the vowel practice has to be extended to include vowel glides. After dealing with consonants individually they can be linked with vowels and sound patterns made.

The second part of word practice is for connected speech. Once the word has been achieved meaning complicates the issue.

VOWEL GLIDE PRACTICE

When making these the aim should be a steady continuous movement of the speech organs resulting in a glide. Success depends on the accuracy of the starting position and the correct direction of the glide.

1. Speak the centring vowel glides rhythmically checking the starting position carefully and experiencing the sensation of movement of the tongue (and lips where applicable)

In unstressed positions and in some regional speech they lose their vowel glide quality and become pure vowels.

H*ERE*
H*AIR*
H*OAR*
T*OUR*

2. Speak the closing vowel glides in the same way.

H*AY*
H*IGH*
H*OW*
H*OY*
H*OE*

Note the movement of the tongue: the rising of the front for H*AY* and H*IGH* but with considerable difference in the length of the glide: the movement from back through centre to front when H*OY* is said: the lip as well as tongue movement in H*OE*.

COMMON FAULTS OF VOWEL GLIDES

(*a*) Two sounds are made instead of a glide.
(*b*) The glide is taken too far with an exaggerated effect.

CONSONANT PRACTICE

The accuracy of consonant formation depends on many factors, among them:

(*a*) The ear.
(*b*) Muscular dexterity of the speech organs.
(*c*) Sensory discrimination of the speech organs.
(*d*) Knowledge of the formation of speech sounds.
(*e*) Early speech education.

The order of importance of these factors varies with each individual.

Consonant practice is often termed ARTICULATION. In a strict sense this means the coming together of two speech organs to make a sound. In a wider way it is used to mean the grouping together of vowels and consonants to make connected speech. ENUNCIATION is a better term for this.

EXERCISES FOR INDIVIDUAL CONSONANTS

1. Ease the jaw.
2. EASE
   STRENGTHEN
   MAKE FLEXIBLE
   GAIN CONTROL of the speech organs making the sound. Exercises for this have been described under Exercises for the Speech Organs (page 38).
3. Make the sound quietly and accurately. Repeat it slowly increasing rate gradually.
4. Repeat the sound making various rhythms.
   kkk*k* kkk*k* kkk*k*
5. Combine the sound with vowels, varying the position.
   kah ahk ahkah
6. Combine the consonant with others in complicated sound patterns.

COMMON FAULTS IN THE ARTICULATION OF INDIVIDUAL SOUNDS

PLOSIVES

Voiced

(*a*) If the sound is over-articulated a short vowel follows the plosion in final position.

(*b*) It should be remembered that voiced plosives in initial and final positions are partially devoiced. Over-voicing them disturbs the balance of the enunciation.

Unvoiced

(*a*) Some speakers make a slight fricative instead of a clean plosion. This is known as AFFRICATION.

Nasals

When the speech organs part before vocalization ceases the nasal is 'released'. This is particularly common in si*ng*. A plosive is often added to this sound in some regional speech.

Laterals

The tip articulation of dark *l* sometimes causes difficulty. Some people use a short back vowel with lip rounding in place of the true alveolar articulation.

Fricatives

(*a*) Too much breath is sometimes used and this is usually combined with weak muscular articulation. The result is an untidy weak sound. Undue length is often added to the fault.
(*b*) the *r* sound suffers from a number of faults. A common fault is the use of an upper teeth lower lip articulation. Another is an *r* made by the back of the tongue and the uvula.
(*c*) *s* has a variety of faults. The most frequent gives the effect of a too low pitched sound: another fault is a high-pitched 'whistly' *s* sound. Poor tongue positioning can give a *sh* or *th* quality.
(*d*) Inability to differentiate between voiced and voiceless sounds results in *f* being substituted for *v* and *th*in for *th*en.

Flapped

Few untrained speakers use flapped *r*. It adds neatness to speech although it should be used with discretion.

Faults in Connected Speech

These are too numerous to list but can be grouped thus:

(*a*) Those due to poor muscular effort resulting in slack weak enunciation.
(*b*) Over-brisk speech of a jerky type.
(*c*) Pronunciation faults arising from poor speech education.

(*d*) Insufficient gradation (sometimes due to a desire to be clear without a teacher's direction).
(*e*) Lack of balance in the speech due to the use of the wrong phonemic variant.
(*f*) Undue lengthening of vowels.
(*g*) No use of the lateral and nasal plosions.

GENERAL PRACTICE FOR THE VOICE

To make the voice a fine flexible instrument final practice must be given in achieving every possible effect with tone and speech. This need not be kept to language but should embrace a range as wide as the apparatus and the imagination allow.

Work should follow these lines:

(*a*) Tone used as widely as possible to include violent noisy passages, lyrical lines, calling, onomatopoeic effects—from fog-horns to musical instruments.
(*b*) The use of the voice in a variety of rooms, halls, theatres and through the microphone.
(*c*) The gaining of dexterity in volume changes.
(*d*) An increasing of the musical value of the voice by ear training with musical instruments and singing. As the range is widened it should be applied in intonation work. Sung phrases should then be spoken aiming at the same notes.
(*e*) Speech rapidity. This should be increased.
(*f*) Words should be brought alive and the full range given zest, from the strong dynamic to the delicate.

CONSONANTS

may be defined as:

	Voicing	Place of Articulation	Manner of Articulation
p	voiceless	bi-labial	plosive
b	voiced	bi-labial	plosive
t	voiceless	alveolar	plosive
d	voiced	alveolar	plosive
k	voiceless	velar	plosive
g	voiced	velar	plosive
*ch*in	voiceless	*palato-alveolar	affricate
*g*in	voiced	*palato-alveolar	affricate
m	voiced	bi-labial	nasal
n	voiced	alveolar	nasal
si*ng*	voiced	velar	nasal
l	voiced	alveolar	lateral
r	voiced	†post-alveolar	frictionless continuant
*th*in	voiceless	dental	fricative
*th*en	voiced	dental	fricative
f	voiceless	labio-dental	fricative
v	voiced	labio-dental	fricative
s	voiceless	alveolar	fricative
z	voiced	alveolar	fricative
*s*ure	voiceless	*palato-alveolar	fricative
mea*s*ure	voiced	*palato-alveolar	fricative
h	voiceless	glottal	fricative
w	voiced	bi-labial	semi-vowel
y	voiced	palatal	semi-vowel

*articulated against the alveolar ridge: friction passes back along the hard palate.
†See page 66.

APPENDIX: ADDITIONAL EXERCISES

Detailed exercises for breath, note, tone and word have been given in the appropriate sections of this book. Material, mostly traditional, for vocal practice and application has been collected in the author's book *Speech Practice* (Pitman). The following ideas and poems may also be useful:

1. Clapping to a rhythm is a way of 'warming up' for a voice practice. As the clapped rhythm is established and energy increases, spoken sounds and words can be introduced.

Try this simple rhythm first. One person taps twice with a pencil on a wooden surface, then everyone claps:

tap tap tap
tap tap tap
tap tap tap
CLAP CLAP CLAP

If a group is taking part, a contra-rhythm can be tried:

CLAP CLAP clap-clap
CLAP

2. George MacBeth has written a clapping poem. It is hard work so the first part only is offered here.

Numerical Analysis of 'Brazilian Poem' from the German of Friederike Mayröcker

(. . . 2 2 6 2 3 6: 2 3 3-6 3 8; 3
6 9 4 8 8; 3 6 10;
9 3 5; 2-2: 5 4 6!
2 10 6 6 (8)—4 3 6 11;
5 6; 8 7; 2 3 6 . . .)
9 5 3 5: 2 3 2
10 4
5 8; 3 9 2 3; 5 3 4 3 3 9 9:(4!)
3 6 3 3 4—9 6; 7
3 3 5; 8; 3 3 6; 10 (3 3 7 4 2 3!)

This looks a puzzle until you realize that each number represents the number of claps to be given. Pause to separate one number from the next. Of course you can use any sound you like instead of, or as well as, claps. Done by a group it has a powerful effect and generates energy besides using it.

3. Another good warming-up ploy is to speak a stanza of a poem as a round. Those with a strongly defined rhythm

There are many ways of playing with this. It falls easily into a four-part arrangement.

are best for the purpose. Here is an example by David Owen-Bell and Angela Konrad.

Once it has been gone through in parts, it's fun if each individual dodges about using words and lines in any way provided the rhythm is kept.

Down by the Mersey
Playing on a bandstand
John, Paul, George
And Ringo Starr

Started as a skiffle group
Then made the big time
Found they could only go
So far.

If four parts are used the ending goes better thus:

go so far
  go so far
    go so far
      found they could only go so far

4. A good noisy example can be releasing vocally and emotionally. The two following poems by David Owen-Bell follow primitive thythms.

Try to let the sounds you are making come from the middle of your being and project them far into the distance.

Call it aloud, aloud, aloud!
Sing it long, long, long!
Words and whisper, whip, whine, whip.
Shout it out, out, out!
Man sits and speaks, man stands and shouts, man convinces.
The words live!

5. This demands maximum use of breath.

Besides loudness, you can enjoy a strong, lifting attack on the words.

The Gale

Twisting me, tearing me,
The knife cuts hard, the flesh withdraws,
Between torn, tormenting terror, gripping
Me, hurting me.

6. Try these scale work-outs arranged by Ernest Joss.

When you can sing it competently, change key.

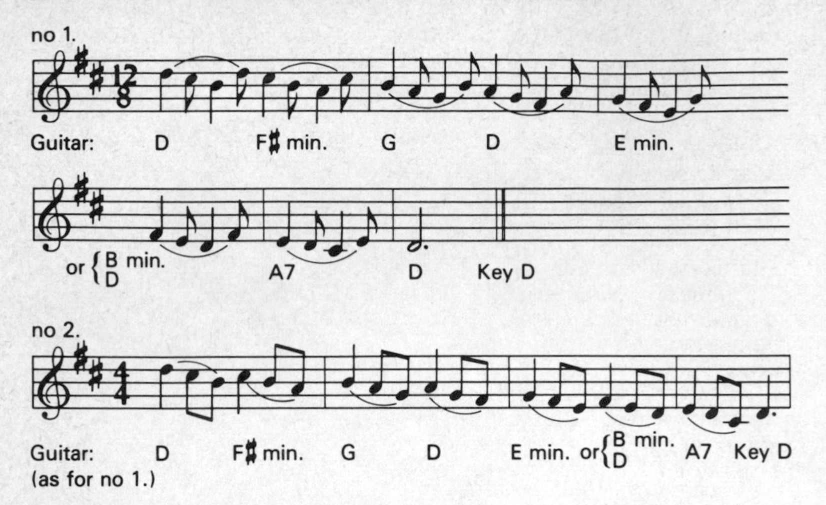

7. The material that follows is a collection of sound poems by Bob Cobbing. There are no rules to follow when interpreting them and this makes them particularly valuable for engendering vocal flexibility. They can be whispered, intoned, sung or spoken as your inclination and imagination dictate.

   There is also freedom in deciding whether they are followed through from beginning to end, or certain lines or words are repeated. If a group is trying them, there is no need for everyone to be active all the time. Shape and meaning are increased if the number speaking at one time varies. The interpretation should be spontaneous and not dictated or rigidly prepared.

Cri Zok

Cri zok cri zok cri zok
Rinkle stammen rinkel stammen
Tak tak tak tak
Gros temps gros temps gros
Temps temps temps temps
Temps terre temps terre
Plume de ma tante

This is an easy one to begin with. Lines can be repeated but as a 'clock' poem. It is very satisfactory just going through from beginning to end.

Tu dors tu dors
To two too door
A door adore
Toc toc toc toc
Tu dors tu dors
Zzzzzz Zzzzzz
Z

(From *ABC in Sound*)

8. *Bombast*

Bombast bombast
Bomb bomb bomb bast
Bombast
Emphase
Em- em- em- phase
Bombast emphase
Bombast
Phébus

(From *ABC in Sound*)

You have to decide for yourself what the sound poems 'mean'. This has been regarded as a clock poem and as a bombardment by different groups working on it. Bob Cobbing often uses French words in his poems so check the pronunciation if you are not certain of it.

9. *La Lune Loop*

Loop
La lune Loop
Ontala ontala tala tala
Low loom Bleep
Bleep la lune Loop
La nuit est morte
Bleep
La lune Loop
Le jour est mort
Ontala tala tala

La loupe
Tala tala
Les runes Droop
Langage
Est mort

(From *ABC in Sound*)

La Lune has been considered to be a study of a dripping tap but it has also been used as a comment on interplanetary travel.

It says something about the death of language in the usual sense and about the birth of a language of sound. It can involve a wide range with high Loops and Bleeps and low ontalas.

10. *Naomi*

naomi imean imoan naomi nioma nioma amoin amion
maino maino oniam oniam moina aniom aniom moina
noami imaon imaon noamo niamo niamo omain omain

miano miano onaim onaim moani inaom inaom moani
noima amion amion noima naimo naimo omian omain
miona miona anoim anoim maoni inoam inoam maoni
maoni inoam inoam maoni miona miona anoim anoim
naimo naimo omian omian noima amion amion noima
moani inaom inaom moani miano miano onaim onaim
niamo niamo omain omain noami imaon imaon noami
moina aniom aniom moina maino maino oniam oniam
nioma nioma amoin amoin naomi imoan imoan naomi

Move about as you wish on this poem with emphasis on the nasals and the vowels. If you have a group working on this, the overall word to emerge will probably be the title word NAOMI.

11. *Ana Perenna*

ana nina na-ana danu una dana
an-anasa nana anu anis ina una
ay mari ramya amarimi rama
enma ira mariamne ariana rana ira
anné ira marienna mirima nana mirim
si tiana ana itis an-athanah tana
hanah-ita ariande ana edna ira ati hanah

an-athanah tana si tiana ana itis
mirima nana mirim anné ira marienna
ariana rana ira enma ira mariamne
amarimi rama ay mari ramya
anu anis ina una an-anasa nana
ana danu una dana ana nina na
(ana danu, una dana, etc)

This one needs delicacy and musicality. You will be surprised at the lyrical achievement that is possible. Each half-line (and the whole poem) is a palindrome and, at the end, it allows for repeats.

12. *Fragment*

sasa kassee jo ook arsaka see
joass sackoo jusoo jaa
ajeck sojooka kee reko sooja jaake
aaeouauueeooeauo
okkuakeko jukokkua aeja reekokussa
saarruu oukekoju
raka jee sseee aajakakee jjeaujok

Plenty of vowel work comes into this. Aim at neatness and accuracy. The ‘j’ should be pronounced as English ‘y’.

ouaeooeeuuauoeaa
sakasee jo ook arsaka see
joassak koojusoo jaa
ajeck sojooka kee
rekosoo ja jaake
aaeouauueeooeauo
okkua keko
juko kua
aoja
ree

13. Insects or birds are the subject of these studies. Give them full onomatopoeic treatment. Stanza 1—frog and lark. Stanza 2—the tse-tse fly and other noxious insects. Stanza 3—crows and others. Stanza 4—chickens, cocks and hens. Stanza 5—doves and pigeons. Stanza 6—a jaunt-about song, which may also be used, whole or in part, between the other stanzas.

1 *kurrirrurriri*
twonk
rol rol rol
twonk twonk
rol rol rol rol
twonk
rol rol rol rol rol
twonk twonk
rol rol rol rol rol rol

2
bubula bubulela
bamberoo bumb-
harali
bomboolios bum-
berooli
tse tse ntsintsi
bumberoo bamb-
harali
bumboolios bam
berooli
tse tse ntsintsi
bomboo bumarali
bulbuluza boozuza
bomboloza zezu

3
kah kah cacak-
djeda
kra kra grika
kra kara kra kacha
kah chacha kah
graji
khrij khrij
kra grika gra
chacha
khrij karat khrij
karot
gra graji grika
chacha
kra klah kah

4
kokro co rico
koklo quiquiriqui
okoko okoka
kuku kukkata
kukko caracaca
kukuk kaluruk
kukuduna kukukasi
kokro coquelicot
koklo tsu koklo no

5
pip
pipio pigione
pippione piccione
pipare
pipire pipiare pigio-
lare pippionare
pippolini pipelni
pipegni
pipay pipok
pip

6
timpa tampa
tump tup
tumbuk timno
tumbak tamno
timpa tampa
tomp tump
tom tom tump tup
tum tum tomp tump

14. This last group is a collection of poems and lines set to music by Ernest Joss. The descant recorder will give a starting note and all the tunes are easy to play. Quavers have been kept in twos and fours to make it easy for beginners in musical notation to grasp the rhythms quickly. When suitable, suggestions for guitar chords have been given.

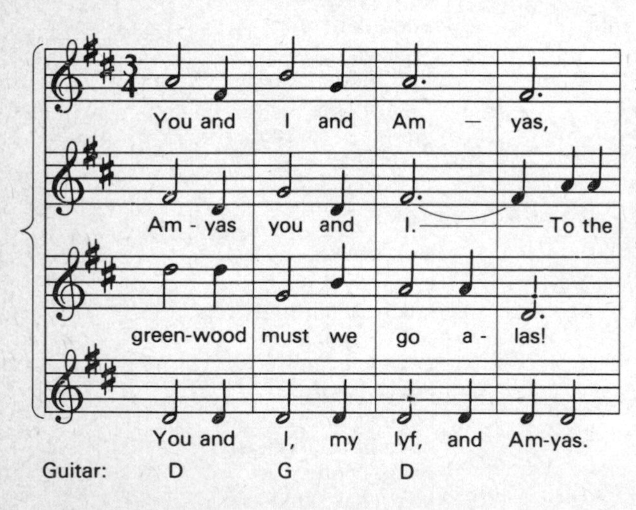

KEY D
Descant recorder.
Tempo and spirit ad libitum.
Learn this as a group warm-up, then sing it as a round.
Finally speak the lines, not necessarily following the tune but using it as a stimulus. The words are a 16th Century snatch, LATET ANGUIS, possibly by William Cornish.

15.

KEY G MINOR
Descant recorder.
Sing this short but sweet round slowly and then speak it.

16.

KEY F
Descant recorder.
A merry, jolly round, good for stimulating vocal energy. Increase the speed when accuracy is certain.

17.

KEY G
Descant recorder.
This should have a contented floating quality. Notice how the lilting tune constrasts unexpectedly with the nonny-nos in the final line. After singing it as a round, speak the lines experimenting with the hey nonnys.

18.

Use this to practise half-tones as a preparation for 19. Sing it, then speak it using half-tones.

19.

KEY D MINOR
Descant recorder. There is no easy guitar to suggest.
It's a fine and difficult round involving chromaticism.
Achieve the mood by singing it 'bravely' against its bitterness of spirit. Carry your gains into an (individually) spoken interpretation of the whole poem (Shakespeare).

20.

KEY D
Descant recorder.
Note carefully the emphases and change of time signature. Choose tempo according to your reaction to the words and your ability.

KEY A
Descant recorder.
Create the breadth of the sky as you sing this, legato. Make sure the jump between B and E in bar 3 is smooth and supported, not jerky and seized back in your throat.
Try a dramatic interpretation of the whole speech. (Milton's masque Comus.)

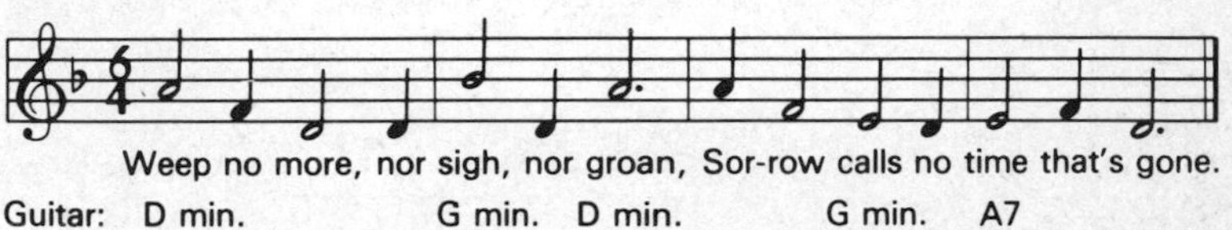

KEY D MINOR
Descant recorder.
Sing it with the simple directive 'with feeling'.

23.

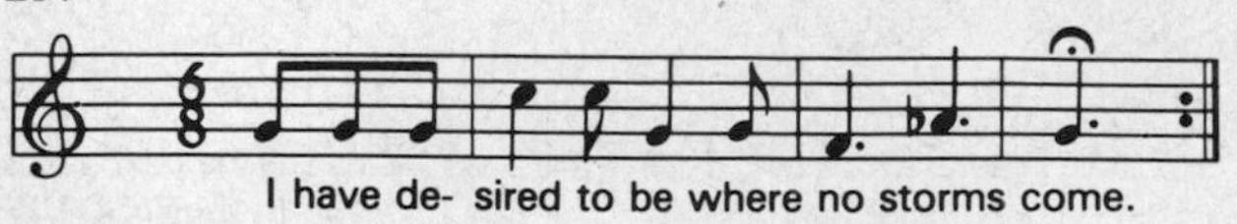

Guitar: C F min. C

KEY C
Use the sung line as a stimulus for speaking the poem Heaven-Haven (Manley Hopkins).

24.

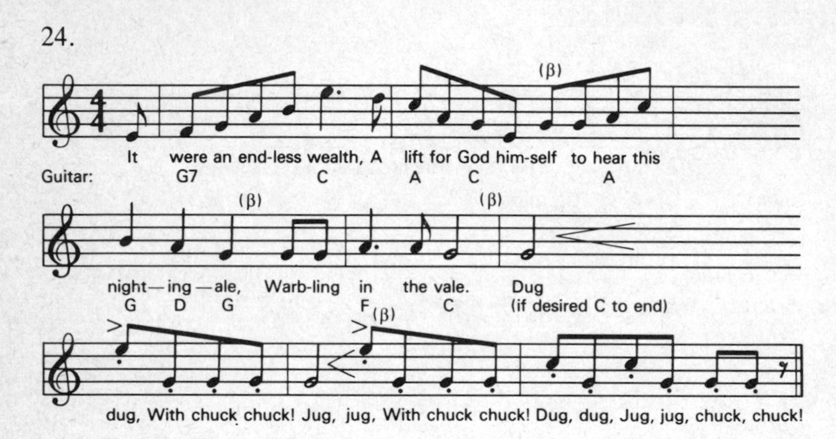

KEY C
Rubato
Make it ecstatic, aiming at a high emotional pitch when speaking it later.
Observe the crescendos and accents. Decide where to breathe. Suggested places are marked β.

NOTES ON VOCAL APPLICATION AND INTERPRETATION

General

There is no gain-saying the primary statement that: UNDERSTANDING—PHYSICAL, INTELLECTUAL AND EMOTIONAL—MUST BE THE PRECURSOR OF PERFORMANCE. The reverse side of this coin 'having a go' is unacceptable. Putting right the wrong first impressions and practice outweighs the little that may be gained. PHYSICAL UNDERSTANDING is the underlined principle of this book. So also is that of THEORY TO PRACTICE. These put to use should enable a speaker to have mastery over his instrument. Having gained this by patient muscular re-education, increased sensory awareness and discrimination and application experience, professional voice users generally sit back satisfied with the job; a few abuse their voices and limp back to their mentors for reconditioning. They ignore the examples of athletes training rigorously, dancers attending a practice class daily, concert pianists making the house resound with scale sounds . . . the list could go on.

Assuming that vocal freedom, strength and flexibility have been achieved and the word is alive in the mouth, further and more subtle vocal experience is in order.

Vocal Practice

Arrange a working area with a mirror and a light enabling you to see what is happening in your mouth. Find a stool, not a chair, the right height for you to keep your length (revise POSTURE, page 18). Before beginning to vocalize, especially if you have not been very active so far that day, do a body work-out selecting movements from PHYSICAL PREPARATION (page 20). Turn your attention to the capacity and control of breath. Ensure a flow of fresh air. Concentrate on thoracic ease, the back lower ribs, full chest breathing and include Rib Reserve if you wish. Enjoy the cool air entering the nose and the warm breath flowing out of the mouth. Direct the airstream towards a distant given point. Link with vocalization. A common fault is to give too much attention to the intake of breath which is then 'hoarded' instead of being used immediately. Air costs nothing so be extravagant with it.

For each practice work round a different idea. For example take any vowel and for fifteen to twenty minutes give it special value.

H*AY*. Exercise the speech organs concentrating on the tongue (pages 39–41). Direct the breath through the H*AR*D H*AY* H*EE*D positions (page 43), then vocalize making tunes with these vowels. Isolate H*AY*. Be sensitive as to what is happening in your mouth as you shape it. Link words—MAY MAY-DAY SHADE WADE STAY RELATE DEDICATE STALE-MATE— and speak them changing rhythm, order, pitch and vocal quality. Spend a couple of minutes on Naomi (page 87, No. 10). Always finish a practice with three or four minutes of direct speech (record yourself—listen and assess it the following day) or by interpreting a poem or prose passage.

Words suggesting strong action stimulate energy: take *GALE-FORCE*. Concentrate on breath capacity and use it without stint. Practice vowels aiming at the impression of the strong wind blowing through them. Be aware of the passage of the vocalized breath as you do this. Work on The Gale (page 85 No. 5; try No. 4 also). Call through a storm from one ship to another.

VOCAL APPLICATION: *Ode to the West Wind* (Shelley) and *Romeo and Juliet*. Capulet, ACT III, Scene V; 'God's breath! it makes me mad:' Keep control, don't shout, but let your voice out on this full-blooded vituperative passage.

Musical instruments are rewarding ideas for tone; DRUMS, VIOLIN, TROMBONE or *FLUTE*. Give attention to H*AR*D H*AW*K H*OO*T (page 43). Image flute music, or listen to some, and let this stimulate pure, cool tone. Sing and speak Additional Exercises, No. 23. Make 'sphere' music. Use *La Lune Loop* (page 87, No. 9).

VOCAL APPLICATION: *The Tempest* (Shakespeare). Any of Ariel's speeches.

From time to time take objective stock of your vocal progress and arrange your practice accordingly.

DEVELOP:

(I) HALF-TONES

Sing and speak Additional Exercises 19 and 20, then choose likely lines and interpret them using half-tones. During the learning process you have to be conscious of your voice. Once skill is gained you should not 'listen' to yourself but let the imagination take over. Half-tones aid lyricism and also help to create off-perspective moods.

VOCAL APPLICATION: *Pied Beauty* (Manley Hopkins). The whole poem lends itself to such interpretation, particularly the line, 'All things counter, original, spare, strange'.

(II) VARIED SPEECH-TUNES

Be adventurous but not outlandish: ensure that you are using speech-tunes acceptable to English (revise page 78). Occasionally sub-mortals or strange beings offer opportunity to do anything you please.

VOCAL APPLICATION: Extend your experience with any scene with Peasblossom, Cobweb, Moth and Mustardseed from *A Midsummer Night's Dream*.

(III) KINETIC TONE

Revise the NUCLEUS (page 77). When a word needs to be emphasized, it is wrong to put weight on it. The right way is to change pitch as the operative syllable is spoken. Link this with oral kinaesthetic sensory discrimination in simple language; feel the word alive in your mouth. When you perform, the listener not only receives what you are saying with his ears but in a slight way he is aware of it orally. Infants learning to speak gain much from the physical energy of those talking to them.

VOCAL APPLICATION. Take any lines of a play or a poem and give them exact significance by use of kinetic syllables.

(IV) A WIDER RANGE

Revise FAULTS OF NOTE (i) and (ii) (page 30). Revise

SCALE WORK-OUT (page 86). Check your range. Begin at a comfortable 'middle' note and speak up from it, then down from it. Squeaking and growling are not of use: the notes must be those you can speak on. Check your informal speaking range—it will probably be rather less than an octave. This increases to about double during performance. Make sure that you can meet exceptional demands: include in these screaming (easy with plenty of breath), crying, moaning and laughing.

(v) RATE SUBTLETY

A few speakers are slow and laboured and may rush and spoil potentially good work. Your physical movement is likely to match your speaking rate: learn from this. Testing your catenation rate, the number of syllables you can articulate accurately but without expression in one minute, is also useful. Take a rhyme you know well. Count the syllables. Find out how many times you can speak it in three minutes. Multiply this by the syllable count. Divide by three. You will then have your catenation rate. If you're a gabbler (i) revise POSTURE (page 18), (ii) bear in mind thought and intention before you speak, (iii) remember the audience needs time to take in what is being communicated. Learn (that means experiment and experience) to be in charge of yourself, your material and your listeners. Subtlety of rate change, nearly always involved with a pause (page 72), renews impetus and keeps performance arresting.

VOCAL APPLICATION. Choose a prose passage. Keep unity of thought and rate as you read it but mark the salient points and slow down just a little to add to their importance. Increase rate slightly over less important passages. Consider also (i) possible climax: time it carefully. (ii) Parentheses: a parenthesis is a phrase within an already complete sentence. Pause before and after it and remove it from the intonation of the main sentence. Change rate on it. (iii) Antitheses: an antithesis is an opposition of thought, usually in two phrases. It needs a slow rate to point it. (iv) First person speech requires a 'thumb-nail' characterization. The 'he said' and so on should be kept in line with it so that there is not an abrupt change. It should be preceded by a pause with interest sustained during it and its rate has to fit the character.

(VI) RHYTHM

Revise the rhythm warm-up (page 84 Nos. 1 and 2) and one or two sung then spoken rounds. Colloquial English varies in rhythm, being individual to the speaker, but has an approximate rhythm of light syllable (˘) and strong syllable (–) grouped in fives (|˘–|˘–|˘–|˘–|˘|). This rising (because the weight is on the second syllable), duple (two syllables to the foot) measure is a common one of English poetry. A good poet varies it by inverting feet and substituting other feet |˘˘| –– |˘˘ –| –˘˘|˘–˘| so adding interest and increasing musical value. Basic rhythmic difficulties are rare but few speakers take full advantage of the variety and impetus it offers.

VOCAL APPLICATION. Try out the marching, galloping, dancing and flying rhymes in *Speech Practice* (Nos. 57, 58, 70, 67, 68). Go on to Gerard Manley Hopkins's sprung (released) rhythm poems and Edith Sitwell's *Façade*.

VOCAL ASPECTS OF INTERPRETATION

Speakers cannot change their physical apparatus, they can only work to make the most of what they have and then apply it with intelligence and imagination. It is a consoling fact that a so-called 'beautiful' voice can quickly become boring. Application has to consider primarily the dictates of acoustic circumstances varying from preachers struggling with vast echoing buildings to actors faced by a microphone. Foreknowledge is the only safeguard. Plant listeners at stations in the church or cavernous theatre and find out where the sound deadens or blares. Estimate volume against projected intensity of tone. If you are a dedicated stage actor, still learn microphone technique and don't be taken by surprise.

Dealing with Texts

NECESSITIES:

(i) Study (thorough)
(ii) Imagination (strong)
(iii) Informed attitude towards language

Item (iii) involves realization of the differences between spoken and written language. Some cultures have a spoken language and a different written one: English covers both aspects but with diversions. We hear the spoken and have to grasp meaning at once; we see the written and may ponder the meaning for as long as we wish. This is as well, as the written has a more complicated syntax and a more difficult vocabulary. The speaker does much of the work for the listener by using intonation and stress to communicate exact meaning and innuendo. So to make the written page come alive it has to be read aloud with grammatical accuracy and far more by way of intonation, fluency (revise phonemic variants, (page 67), elision (page 70), gradation (page 71), assimilation (page 70)) and with a telling vocal quality. The voice by intention plus skill conveys far more than meaning: try out (*a*) two or three characters: build them with care, detail them, seek points of identification, experience them at second hand, respect the dramatist and hold the audience; (*b*) several strong emotional situations; (*c*) poems of varying moods. In dealing with (*c*) some knowledge of verse form is needed. It is worth remembering also how much traditional drama, still played today, is in blank verse. Revise pause and the caesura (page 72) and rhythm (page 99).

FURTHER POINTS

PRIMARY RHYTHM is that of the foot |˘–|, SECONDARY RHYTHM is that of the line (number of feet) and TERTIARY is that of the stanza (how many lines?) Choose a sonnet: this has a water-tight form having five rising duple feet to fourteen lines. Attention to the rhyme scheme will help you when you speak it. Make sure that you give each line its five feet: it is easy to say some with four only, but this not only breaks the form but can alter the

Alexander Technique

14. *The Alexander Principle*, by Wilfred Barlow (Victor Gollancz, 1973).

Interpretation

15. *Drama Skills*, by Greta Colson (Barrie and Jenkins, 1980).

line's significance. Note the foot variations: the first of a line (|˘–|) is often reversed (|–˘|) to give a strong opening. Blank verse has five rising duple feet (|˘–|˘–|˘–|˘–|˘–|), no rhyme and goes on and on to the end of the speech. Choose a fairly long speech from a Shakespeare part you might play and analyse its form (inverted and substituted feet and whether the lines are enjambed). Such study adds extra security and occasionally illuminates meaning. Once you have mastered the form, you can forget it as such. This goes for all the technical advice given in this book. Learn the job, keep up your practice, and be free to respond to your creative power and inspiration.

BIBLIOGRAPHY

INTONATION

1. *Intonation of Colloquial English*, by J. D. O'Connor & G. F. Arnold (Longmans, Green, 1961). Records spoken by the authors are available.
2. *The Groundwork of English Intonation*, by Roger Kingdon (Longmans, Green, 1958).
3. *An English Intonation Reader*, by W. R. Lee (Macmillan, 1960). Records spoken by the author are available.
4. *English Intonation Practice*, by Roger Kingdon (Longmans, Green, 1958).

(Phonetic transcription is not used in any of the above except as an additional item in No. 3. All the books may be read and understood fully without a knowledge of phonetic notation.)

VOICE AND SPEECH: GENERAL

5. *Cunningham's Text-Book of Anatomy*, edited by Brash (Oxford Medical Publications).
6. *The Respiratory Muscles*, by E. J. Moran Campbell (Lloyd-Luke).
7. *Living Anatomy*, by R. D. Lockhart (Faber).
8. *The Mechanism of the Larynx*, by V. E. Negus (Heinemann).

PRONUNCIATION

9. *An English Pronouncing Dictionary*, by Daniel Jones (Dent).
10. *Chambers Twentieth Century Dictionary* (Chambers).
11. *The Shorter Oxford English Dictionary*, (2 vols), (Oxford University Press).
12. *An Introduction to the Pronunciation of English*, by A. C. Gimson (Edward Arnold, 1962).
13. *Practical Phonetics*, by J. C. Wells & Greta Colson (Pitman).

INDEX